Robert J. Rivera

D0571577

Knowledge
Acquisition
for
Expert
Systems

Knowledge Acquisition for Expert Systems

Anna Hart

McGraw-Hill Book Company

New York   St. Louis   San Francisco   Montreal   Toronto

Library of Congress Cataloging-in-Publication Data

Hart, Anna.
    Knowledge acquisition for expert systems.

    Bibliography: p.
    Includes index.
    1. Expert systems (Computer science) 2. Artificial
intelligence. I. Title.
QA76.76.E95H37   1986   006.3'3   86-14380
ISBN 0-07-026909-2

Copyright © 1986 by Anna Hart. All rights reserved.
Printed in the United States of America. Except as permitted
under the United States Copyright Act of 1976, no part of this
publication may be reproduced or distributed in any form or by
any means, or stored in a data base or retrieval system, without
the prior written permission of the publisher.

    234567890   DOC/DOC   89321098

ISBN 0-07-026909-2

First published in Great Britain in 1986 by Kogan Page Ltd.

First American edition published by McGraw-Hill in 1986.

Printed and bound by R.R. Donnelley & Sons Company.

Contents

Preface

My interest in expert systems started a couple of years ago.
I had previously been sceptical about the term 'artificial
intelligence': sceptical about what had been achieved and
indeed what could be achieved. However, some of the
practical developments in expert systems seemed exciting
and useful. Many of the projects are simple in comparison
with strict artificial intelligence: it is more relevant that
they are useful. Since then I have seen the development of
several projects. In my discussions with other researchers
people have asked 'Why don't you write that down?' Their
comments were usually in the context of knowledge
acquisition, which is still a major problem. Encouraged by
their comments I set about the daunting task of putting my
findings and ideas into this book.

As soon as you start to write things down you realize
how little you actually know. I am heartened that worthier
men than I have made this comment in the preface to their
books. Very few people have tackled the problem of writing
about knowledge acquisition. This is hardly surprising,
because the current state of the art is ill-defined and at a
stage of experimentation and evolution. However, I believe
that ideas should be written down, even if they subsequently
prove to be inadequate. Let us have something from which to
work. So this humble work represents my thoughts on the
subject. It is an overview which draws together ideas from
several disciplines. It is not complete: I do not believe that
it could be. I trust that it is not misleading or incorrect.
The reader should treat it as a collection of ideas,
suggestions and problems, not a definitive text. If it is all
merely 'common sense' then that is good; if it contains some
ideas which are more than common sense and which help the

reader to tackle knowledge acqusition more confidently and effectively then it is a success. If it leads him to follow up a reference to a more detailed exposition of a technique then it has been useful. Most of the methods mentioned appear in other disciplines: this text brings them together.

The scope of the work is knowledge acquisition. I do not make a clear distinction between knowledge acquisition and knowledge elicitation: some people do. I have not covered the area of knowledge representation. This was deliberate. It is covered adequately elsewhere, and duplication of material would not enhance this book. On the other hand, one of the messages of the book is that the knowledge engineer should not pre-judge how the knowledge is to be represented until a fair amount of knowledge acquisition has taken place. However, the inference mechanism seems to me to be one of the major problems. I am not entirely happy with the methods which are widely used, although I cannot at present suggest a more excellent and general approach. I do believe that there are difficulties with rules and probabilities, and so some chapters touch on these issues. The overall problem is that computers process numbers very easily: human beings do not. Judgement under uncertainty has been a research area in psychology for several years. Expert system development resurrects the arguments in a slightly different context, but does not answer the questions.

My mood varies, and from time to time the reader will note variations of optimism and pessimism in these pages. Computers and expert system techniques present exciting challenges, but there have been extravagant claims and some reluctance to evaluate and test some of the systems which have been produced. The methods are not fool-proof. Expert systems are here for our use, not vice versa. I am saddened to see that some projects are carried out for the fame of the researcher rather than for practical benefit. The work should be of benefit, and the project should be tackled sensibly: too many people have ignored well-established methods for the sake of something 'new'.

Perhaps one of the main benefits from this kind of research is an improved understanding of the expertise both by the expert and others. Knowledge elicitation can be useful in its own right. The techniques in this book can be of great benefit even if the project does not culminate in a working expert system. For this reason I encourage people to tackle such projects.

Much of the material is anecdotal, and based on hours of discussion with friends in industry. I thank them all for their help and encouragement. Examples in the book are based on real ones, but should be taken as illustrative and not the verified results of experiment. They must not be taken as statements of policy or recognized procedure because many of them are specifically designed to illustrate a particular feature or problem. For reasons of confidentiality I am not able to use data from some applications with which I have been involved.

I thank those who have encouraged me to write, and those who have made helpful comments on draft material: I hope that you are not disappointed. This work would not have been possible without the continued support of my mother and my husband who never fail me. Now that it is completed the volume is dedicated to my fan club of Sarah and Andrew. I thank Anne for her careful and patient typing, and everybody for enduring my bad temper. May these pages stimulate the reader to better things.

Anna Hart
February 1986

As in classical languages, the pronoun 'he' is assumed to embrace both genders. I do not consider it necessary to break up sentences by the continual reminder that we were made male and female.

CHAPTER 1

The nature of expertise

'Can machines think?' is a question that has been argued
about since the very early days of Charles Babbage and
Lady Lovelace. The argument that computers can do only
what they are told to do is countered by 'We don't fully
know what we can tell them to do'. Workers in artificial
intelligence (AI) have been the subjects of both admiration
and scorn. Views about the desirability of making machines
think have ranged from impossible to undesirable to
inevitable. Predictions made in the 1950s about the rate of
development of AI have proved false, and the arguments rage
on — many of them being emotional or ethical (Feigenbaum
& McCorduck 1984; Michie & Johnston 1985; Yazdani
& Narayanan 1984). At a trivial level, if thought is defined as
something biological, then almost by definition a machine
cannot think. In a sense, however, the debate is futile. It is
far more useful to concentrate on what machines *can* do,
and how this can be used to our benefit. It is undeniably true
that current programs are capable of performing spectacular
tasks with a high level of achievement — a far cry from the
early number-crunching programs.

Intelligence
It is not easy to define intelligence. We find it easier to
recognize than to define. Although there are metrics like the
intelligence quotient, it is often rated subjectively. Arguments
abound about intelligence and whether it is peculiar to *homo
sapiens*. Some maintain that animals can display intelligence,
and others go so far as to say that plants also exhibit a form
of intelligence. What computers *can* do is to mimic or
simulate intelligence. Nowadays, they can be made to
perform tasks which would require 'intelligence' if carried

out by a human being. In specific areas, computers can behave like humans: whether or not this constitutes 'thought' is a secondary issue. What is reasonably well agreed is that intelligence is associated with handling knowledge: intelligence is a specialization of knowledge (Lehrer 1974; Osborn 1953). A person's intelligence is measured not merely by what he knows, but by what he can do with it, i.e. the way in which he uses and applies that knowledge. The area of AI which has had most practical impact is that of *intelligent knowledge based systems (IKBS)*, or *expert systems*. These are programs which perform tasks which are usually performed by experts: they embody expert knowledge and the ability to use that knowledge to solve problems. These programs are restricted in the types of tasks they can perform, but in approaching suitable problems they demonstrate expertise (Elithorn & Banerji 1984). Knowledge is encoded within such programs, and therefore they are powerful tools.

Experts

It is very easy to make a list of people who might be thought of as experts. Such a list might include specific names of individuals, or professions of people who, by virtue of their status, would be expected to be experts. People will tend to respect them, trust them, and believe what they say. In short, we assume that they know what they are talking about! Such conclusions about experts can be reached in two ways:

> *Personal experience* — we may have consulted them, or know them personally, and have found that they give correct or helpful advice and solve problems satisfactorily.

> *Reputation and standing* — they may have been recommended by other people; or they may have a good reputation. We might have seen them on television, or read their books. Alternatively, they may hold a position of high responsibility and if they were not experts then they would not be able to maintain credibility in such a position.

In short, experts are experts because of what they are able to do with their acquired knowledge. It might be useful to consider a few examples of experts, and the way they are invaluable to us.

14

DOCTOR

We have to be able to trust a doctor's judgement. A good doctor is able to diagnose and help. He listens sympathetically and carefully, asks relevant questions, takes notice of what we tell him and then diagnoses an illness which satisfactorily explains the symptoms. He then prescribes a course of treatment to ease or cure the illness. When appropriate he gives us a clear explanation of what we can and cannot do, and how to administer the course of treatment. We begin to distrust a doctor and doubt his expertise if he proves to be unable to help or diagnose. If the complaint is difficult to diagnose then we expect him to be able to recognize this and seek specialist help from a more renowned expert in a specialist area.

CAR MECHANIC

If we trust our car to a mechanic then we expect him to be competent at diagnosing faults, and carrying out repairs. A garage gets a good reputation if its mechanics are reliable and if they carry out the necessary work efficiently.

TEACHER

Teachers should be experts at their subjects. They should convey facts and information effectively to their students. A good teacher knows how to express himself at the level and speed appropriate to his students. He will answer questions, and work through examples. Students have confidence in a teacher who is familiar with his material and can consistently solve problems and explain how the answer is achieved. Students have little confidence in a teacher who gets stuck repeatedly and needs to refer to a book, or who fends off questions.

SOLICITOR

The complexities of the legal world are almost unintelligible to the layman. A country's law comprises hundreds of details, sub-details, clauses and exceptions, all written in legal terminology. Any legal document should be written in the correct language, and obey the appropriate rules. Even a will, which conceptually may be simple, must conform to these rules; otherwise it may not mean what you intended it to mean, or it may be totally invalid. If a solicitor helps to draw up such a document then we expect him to be familiar with the relevant legal aspects, and know where to find further details which are pertinent to our case. He should be able to understand our case, extract all the information he needs — including that which we had not thought of — and translate all this into a correct format. We have to trust that he is able to do this, and so we consult a family solicitor from whom we have had efficient and effective service, or one recommended by friends. We expect that an ineffective solicitor would acquire a poor reputation, and soon run out of clients.

The role of experts

Experts have a body of knowledge which is unfamiliar to the layman. Furthermore, they have a proven track-record of being able to use that knowledge (Goodall 1985). They are characterized by the following features:

Effectiveness — the expert can use his knowledge to solve problems, with an acceptable rate of success. The doctor can make correct diagnoses, and the solicitor can identify the appropriate subset of the law.

Efficiency — it is not sufficient to be able merely to solve problems; an expert can solve them quickly and efficiently. He can deduce more probable solutions and quickly determine the most relevant information. A car mechanic who takes a week to determine a simple fault on a car is inefficient, and we would not want to pay him for his labour! We do not want to have to undergo dozens of irrelevant tests at a hospital before a doctor finally realizes what is wrong with us. Difficult problems take longer to solve than straightforward ones, but the expert is characterized by his insight into a problem.

Awareness of limitations — an expert knows what he knows. He is aware of what he is able to deal with, and what needs referring to someone else. We do not respect teachers who pretend to know answers. It is reasonable that they do not know everything about their subject, and that they appreciate when a question is too complex for them. We do not want them to guess at an answer, and give us inaccurate information. If the solicitor is not sure of a

point of law we hope that we would consult someone who
would be familiar with details. A general practitioner who
always refers us to a hospital consultant is ineffective, but
we would want to be referred to a specialist if we had a
serious illness. The doctor should be able to recognize the
symptoms of a disease which is beyond his scope.

We now have some idea of what constitutes an expert. It is
appropriate now to summarize the ways in which we use
experts:

As a provider of information — The expert has a great deal
of knowledge readily available to him. Sometimes we need
certain items of information. We may discuss hypothetical
cases, or ask him questions about details. We can use an
expert like we would a text book with a question-answer
facility, where his answer meets our particular requirements,
and is phrased in terms which we can understand.

As a problem-solver — Using his knowledge an expert can
solve problems. Given sufficient evidence or symptoms he
can easily identify possible or probable solutions. He can
also describe the extra information that would be needed
in order to come to more definite conclusions.

As an explainer — Sometimes the answer on its own is
insufficient. The expert should be able to explain his line
of reasoning and how he came to his conclusion. He should
be able to amplify definitions. When consulting him, we
may ask for explanations for several reasons. These include
learning — to increase our knowledge we might ask 'How
did you know that?'. Alternatively, we might be
confidence building. 'Why do you need to know that?'
would be a reasonable question if he asked for sensitive
or personal information. Information will be divulged only
if the expert's competence is accepted.

In general, consultation with an expert may involve a mix of
all these modes. As the two (or more) people interact there is
a general exchange of information and knowledge. An expert
will also be versatile and able to make a sensible judgement
about the type of answer or detail that is required. When we
consult an expert then we have certain intentions and
expectations; an expert can tailor his information to meet

individual, specific needs. Sometimes this involves a one-word answer, and sometimes a lengthy explanation. On other occasions we might want to suggest solutions and listen to his comments and criticisms. Some experts may listen while we talk through our problem, making an occasional helpful comment to assist us. In many consultations the 'non-expert' contributes to at least half the dialogue.

Summary

Arguments about what constitutes artificial intelligence are, in practical terms, of little merit. Experts are people who have acquired and are able to use certain types of knowledge. There are various ways in which we use experts. When we consult an expert we do not want a catalogue of his knowledge; rather, we need some specific information to solve a particular problem. True experts are able to use their knowledge to give us acceptable answers to particular problems.

CHAPTER 2
Programs as experts

Our industry and economy, our health and safety, depend on experts; or more accurately, on knowledge. In knowledge lies power: power to inform, to decide, and to control. There are now attempts being made to produce intelligent machines endowed with large amounts of knowledge, together with knowledge-handling facilities. If knowledge is contained within computers then it becomes a commodity which can be sold (Feigenbaum & McCorduck 1984). The importance of knowledge as a resource inspires people to build expert systems. Expert computer systems could have distinct advantages over human experts (Michie & Johnston 1985).

Definition of expert systems
An expert system could be defined as (Welbank 1983):

> An expert system is a program which has a wide base of knowledge in a restricted domain, and uses complex inferential reasoning to perform tasks which a human expert could do.

In a practical context, one of the important features of an expert system is the capability of explanation. In the same way that a human expert should be able to explain his conclusions and reasoning, an expert system should be capable of concise or detailed explanations. Apart from this being one of the characteristics of experts, there are other reasons why explanation is important. The legal, ethical or moral aspects of decision-making still remain with humans, and so justification of an answer is an important part of a system's output. At the present time expert systems are used to aid decision-making, and not to take the full responsibility for it. In some, perhaps all, domains this seems desirable. Expert systems should therefore be viewed as tools for use by humans.

The two main features of expert systems which distinguish them from ordinary computer programs are that they:

1) use heuristics,
2) are data driven, and not procedure driven.

Experts do not merely follow a set of rules. They have insight into problems and are able to use their professional judgement. Experts generally use heuristics rather than algorithms. In an algorithm a goal (or type of answer) is assumed, and a series of steps carried out which leads to that goal. Brain problems require a solution which is 'adequate' and not necessarily 'the answer'. Expertise includes the ability to choose a best path from various possibilities, using the best stimuli from several available. Insight is the ability to perceive meaningful relationships; these can be between events or evidences which are usefully but not necessarily logically related. There are no rules for such an approach. The process involves weighing up the potential outcome of different paths and comparing them with the goal; those which seem to lead to states near the goal are considered to be worth pursuing. If a promising path leads to a dead-end then it may be necessary to go back, or back-track, and try a different alternative (Johnson-Laird & Wason 1977; Lehrer 1974; Puff 1982; Osborn 1953). Such methods are inspired guesses, or rules of thumb, called *heuristics*.

Experts work using available evidence. This may be provided by a client with a problem who gives the expert all the available facts or data. Based on these data, the expert will then ask further questions and will eventually reach a conclusion about the problem. An expert system must, therefore, be able to respond to external stimuli. The path that it takes and the ensuing outcome are very much dependent on the data provided.

Advantages of using expert systems
Traditional computer programs have advantages over manual systems, and with well-produced expert systems the advantages could be similar (Alty & Coombs 1984; Goodall 1985). The main ones are:

Availability: Experts are not born. They have to be trained and then practise. It generally takes over five years for someone to acquire expertise in a particular area. The facts given in books are only a skeleton for knowledge. The practitioner learns from years of experience of dealing with different cases, and learning patterns and principles which really are heuristics or guidelines. These are seldom documented. *Declarative knowledge*, or the facts, is relatively easy to acquire; the *procedural knowledge*, or how to use those facts, is far more complex.

A trainee working with an expert takes some time to reach his superior's level of expertise. If the expert's knowledge could be encoded into an expert system then several versions of that system could be made available in a short period of time. In contrast to the human the program would not get tired or irritable, would not take holidays, it would not become ill, and would not die. The knowledge could also be made more readily available to trainee experts or users.

Consistency: Even the best human expert can have an 'off' day, when he is not feeling well. He can make mistakes or may forget an important point. With a good expert system mistakes will be rare, but nonetheless they will occur. A program is consistent. Provided that it is correctly formulated then it will be consistently correct. Apart from hardware failures, there is no reason why a program should lose information or behave oddly. Once a program is right, it is right consistently. The problem in developing expert systems is getting the program 'right' and having the confidence that it is right and ready for use.

Comprehensiveness: It is very difficult to get the joint opinion of more than one expert, and to get a group of experts to discuss a case and reach a concensus opinion is almost impossible. An expert can only draw upon his own knowledge and experience. With a computer system there is no reason why an expert system could not encapsulate the knowledge of more than one expert, so that its decision-making was at least as good as any of the individual contributors. Alternatively, expert systems could consult with each other, and offer several options. Much of this remains in the future, and represents an optimistic view when compared with achievements to date, but some systems have been developed which contain knowledge from more than one source.

21

Interest in expert systems has grown at a terrific rate over the past few years. In general, the most successful developments have been those with modest objectives, taking about six months to produce. There are two types of areas where expert systems are suitable:

1) Problems with a large number of possible combinations, which would take a very long time to sift through.
2) Interpreting large amounts of signal data, or performing *information retrieval*.

How are expert systems different?

Many people wonder how expert systems differ from more conventional programs: What makes the expert system expert? (Elithorn & Banerji 1984; O'Shea & Eisenstadt 1984; Rich 1984; Winston 1984). There is a variety of software available on the market, some of which is very complex. An interesting, if controversial question is 'What is special about an expert system?'. There are cases of projects which have been carried out to develop expert systems where at the start of the project the task was thought to be very complex. However, after extensive knowledge acquisition and refinement systems have been produced which are conceptually simple. In a sense it has been the knowledge acquisition which has been difficult, and not the subsequent implementation. Are such programs, whose structure is relatively simple, expert systems or programs solving complex problems? Really the question is irrelevant in the context of this book, because the prime concern here is with knowledge acquisition. We are interested in producing useful programs, and what they are called is, to some extent, a secondary issue.

Despite differences of opinion, there are fairly well-defined expectations of expert systems (Alty & Coombs 1984; Hayes Roth, Waterman & Lenat 1983; Michie 1982). They must have knowledge, together with some means of handling that knowledge. Clearly, they must also be able to communicate with users. A model of the basic elements of an expert system is shown in Figure 2.1, and it can be seen to comprise:

1) The *knowledge base*, which contains a representation of the knowledge that is required.
2) The *inference mechanism*, which is the means by which this knowledge is handled.

3) The *input/output interface*, which enables the user to supply facts and data, and enables the system to ask questions or supply advice and explanation.

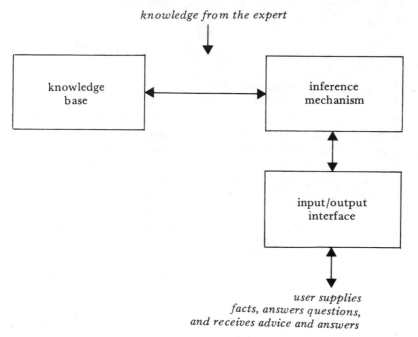

Figure 2.1 *The main parts of an expert system are the knowledge base and inference mechanism which handle the knowledge, and an interface to allow a user to access that knowledge.*

Some authorities prefer the term knowledge-based systems to expert systems. However, this also includes user interfaces, robotic systems, etc. It is the knowledge that is included in the program which gives it its power, and not the particular mechanism or representation which is used. This book addresses the problem of acquiring that knowledge in order to make the program powerful.

History of expert systems development
It is possible to write an expert system in a computer language such as PASCAL or FORTRAN, making use of database facilities if required. However, certain special languages have features which make them particularly suitable for AI work

(O'Shea & Eisenstadt 1984; Rich 1984; Winston 1984).
LISP was invented by John McCarthy in 1958, and has
become a very important language for most AI researchers.
LISP is based on the idea of lists, and list processing. In fact,
list structures are its only data types. Furthermore, a LISP
program consists of functions defined in a mathematical
format, and not a sequence of steps.

PROLOG is a language which is designed to handle logic.
It is a *declarative language* based on formal logic, which
allows the user to state facts about a problem and the
interrelationships between those facts. A problem is 'solved'
by querying the resultant database of information. There are
other languages which are frequently used in AI work, such
as PLANNER, SAIL and FUZZY.

An alternative to programming 'from scratch' is to use an
expert system shell (Alty & Coombs 1984; Goodall 1985).
A famous example of a shell is EMYCIN, derived from
MYCIN. A shell is an expert system emptied of its knowledge
base, leaving the inference mechanisms and user interface.
Provided that the structure is appropriate, the shell can hold
a different set of domain knowledge to provide a different
expert system. There are a few of these available
commercially; their major advantage is that their use can
save time during system development. A disadvantage is that
they can be very restrictive, unless the inference mechanisms
in the various domains are almost identical. If the knowledge
has to be contorted to go into the shell, then the results will
be very poor.

Tools are now being produced, based on languages and
shells, for use in expert system development. What is available
will generally depend on the language capabilities of the
computer system being used.

Applications of expert systems and some examples
Expert systems have been developed for the following tasks
(Feigenbaum & McCorduck 1984; Alty & Coombs 1984;
Goodall 1985): interpretation of laws or rules, diagnosis of
illness or fault diagnosis, debugging, corrosion analysis,
design, and planning. Some of the better known systems are
described below:

DENDRAL — This is one of the earliest applications of AI
techniques to real problems. It interprets mass

spectographs, to determine a molecule's structure and also its atomic constituents.

MYCIN — A very famous system which diagnoses meningitis and blood infections, and recommends treatment.

PROSPECTOR — This is used in prospecting for mineral ore; it helps to identify probable sites for good deposits.

RI or XCON — A commercially used expert system which configures VAX computer systems.

PROGRAMMER'S APPRENTICE — Assists programmers in the tasks of software construction and debugging.

TAXMAN — A system to interpret tax laws and suggest arrangements that can be chosen to meet financial objectives.

Problems of using expert systems

The tone of this chapter has been fairly optimistic about the potential of expert systems. However, the explosion in interest together with extravagant claims made by some researchers tend to give a false perspective of the true state of the art of expert systems development. There are a number of areas which need consideration if a system is to be useful (Yazdani & Narayanan 1984); these include:

Choice of domain — Some problems are too complex to be served by expert systems. If experts disagree, or a specialist in the domain is not available, then the domain is unsuitable. Similarly, so too are problems which take a long time (more than a few hours) to solve, where there are many interactions, or there is a lot of dependence on spatial relationships, procedures or commonsense concepts.

Acceptability — Not everyone wants to rely on a computer, or even use one; some people have a resistance to their use and would prefer to deal with human experts. Even the experts are sometimes sceptical about expert systems. This is true even when the systems are performing well and in agreement with the experts, since they feel that the programs cannot be using the same sorts of reasoning as they do.

25

Uncertainty — Much of the data handled by experts is uncertain, and data may be missing. The way in which expert systems handle uncertainty tends to be rather *ad hoc*. In fact, this has resulted in severe criticism of the way in which probability theory has been used, and the apparent dismissal of other well-established techniques.

Updating — Domains where the knowledge is changing frequently are not well suited to expert system development. The knowledge base will need updating if the expert system is to retain its expertise. The facilities for updating knowledge bases could be improved.

Limitations — A human expert knows his limitations. As yet expert systems do not perform very well in this respect. They tend always to produce an answer and thus there is a general tendency to over-diagnose. This can be problematic, and it should be stressed that they are most sensibly used as tools to assist rather than to replace.

Testing — Many 'traditional' computer systems are put into operation without being fully tested. 'Bugs' are often found on-site while the programs are in operation. Testing an expert system presents real problems. Developers are not always sure about how systems should behave, and so they cannot test them thoroughly. It is not easy to define the paths through an expert system program, and it is very difficult to test for completeness or correctness. This is especially serious in applications where high risk is involved (for instance, medical applications). Testing and maintaining a system becomes increasingly difficult when the size of the system is increased.

Behaviour — Although the aim of an expert system is that it should imitate a human expert, there are very few which actually do this. Dialogues are usually directed by the program, and explanations can often be difficult to understand. Consultations tend to be program driven and not user driven, and the user often has to suffer unnecessary explanation or output in order to obtain an answer.

Knowledge acquisition — The rest of this book will be addressed to this problem. All the knowledge must be acquired before it can be represented, and it is this area which is restricting expert systems development at present.

Why use expert systems?

An expert system should be useful and be produced to serve a need. Most of the successful systems in use at present (apart from the pioneering systems mentioned earlier) are *rule-based* programs that perform tasks which could be regarded as rather tedious. Many of these could be summarized as sophisticated forms of information retrieval systems. Successful systems tend to use relatively simple techniques, and the main advantage of their use is that they enable knowledge to be represented and made more readily available.

Summary

Exaggerated claims have produced some very ambitious aims for expert systems. Computer programs do have advantages in many respects, being able to perform tasks that are normally difficult or tedious, and therefore they can be very useful tools in business and industry. Most of the expert systems in operation at present are problem-solving programs which require the coding of knowledge into the program. Currently, programs do not imitate human experts; they are not as versatile, and they are not aware of their limitations. It is unlikely and undesirable that programs should completely replace human experts, but they can be used very successfully as tools to assist them.

CHAPTER 3

Systems analysis – a comparison

'A decision is only as good as the information on which it is based' is a perfectly good maxim for managers. A similar one in knowledge engineering might be 'An expert system is only as good as the knowledge which is in it', and this implies the knowledge which has been elicited from the expert or experts. More familiarly, in computing, one could say that a system design is no better than the systems analysis which has preceded it. In fact, any design and implementation must be based on information which is complete and correct. It is also true that the extraction and formulation of this information is often more difficult than the subsequent designing or decision-making processes. *Systems analysis* is the process whereby a system is evaluated and analysed, often with a view to computerizing some or all of it.

Systems analysis has been developed over a number of years, and some formal methodologies have evolved. There is a multitude of text books on the subject (for instance see Gane & Sarson 1979) and no shortage of prescriptive literature on the procedures involved. However, projects continue to fail, sometimes with disastrous results. Some systems take years to develop as errors are weeded out and then 'fixed' one by one. There are distinct analogies between systems analysis and knowledge elicitation. Before considering the extra complexities involved in expert systems development, some important points become evident in a study of the pitfalls which exist in systems analysis.

Overview of systems analysis
The main stages in systems development are as follows:

Project selection — Ideas for different projects are evaluated, and the one to be developed is chosen.

Feasibility study — This provides a cost-benefit analysis of alternative approaches to a particular project. It also provides a more detailed definition of the work to be undertaken, and defines the main requirements and features of the system.

Analysis — The systems analysis follows on from the preliminary results of the feasibility study, and provides a basis for the design. It requires a detailed study and evaluation of the current system. All requirements, constraints and objectives should be documented and discussed fully. The analysis should provide a model of the new system in terms of data storage and data flow, inputs and outputs.

Design — The design involves taking the logical model of 'what' is to be done, and preparing detailed technical specifications of 'how' this is to be achieved using the available hardware. Documents are produced for the computer specialists.

Development and testing — Programs have to be written, files created and stationery produced. User documentation must be written and staff trained. All aspects of the system should be thoroughly tested to verify that they conform to the original specifications.

Changeover and use — Once the system has been tested thoroughly the changeover from the old system can take place. This is a strictly controlled procedure. Only after commissioning is complete can the system be used.

This analysis stage is fundamental to good systems design. All necessary questions should be asked and resolved before the design stage or, at the very latest, the implementation stage. The later a mistake or omission is discovered the more severe are its effects. It can be costly to correct, and will almost certainly involve going through several stages in the development a second time. These errors are often attributed to negligence on the part of the systems analyst. This is not always true. The analyst must use many inter-personal and communications skills and deal effectively with the many different people with whom he works. In attempting to bridge the gap between the computer technology and the user's domain he is marrying together two quite different worlds. Clearly, it is very important that all the necessary issues are discussed in adequate detail at the analysis stage.

A CASE STUDY — A HORROR STORY!
Consider the following extract from a conversation which is based on a real incident. Mistakes that have occurred in the systems analysis will become evident as the scene develops.

Sarah   Oh no, not all that again!

Mr Heath I'm afraid so. Apparently, they can't solve the problem — or bug — unless an analyst comes over to see us again.

Sarah   That Dr Bailey fellow who came before?

Mr Heath No, a different one. He's the same sort of person, but coming to cross-check. You've nothing to worry about: just answer the questions as best you can.

Sarah   But that's exactly what I did before. In fact, I told that Bailey several times over. He couldn't follow what I said. He just didn't understand about the log sheets. He just about got how to fill them in, but he couldn't grasp what it was all about, and why some are exceptions. He said he'd understood and then asked a question which showed that he hadn't. And he kept going on about the legislation. Were laws about tachographs likely to change in the near future? Well how do I know?

Mr Heath But he got most of the information — we've got the programs. They reckon it was just one small point he missed which fouls up the way they've designed it all.

Sarah   Oh I know all about that. It was that business about drivers changing lorries. He asked me whether they changed frequently and I said no.

Mr Heath That's right.

Sarah   Aha! But for a computer once a month is frequently. The programs think that not frequently is once in a blue moon, and so every time one changes it makes an hour's work for me. Each time gets worse, and according to that long-haired programmer fellow we can't keep on doing it for ever.

Mr Heath Well this time make sure he knows all the details.

Sarah   I thought I had. I told him the rest at least three times. He doesn't speak the same language. To start with I thought an analyst was a chemist, and then he spent ages talking about fields and characters or something. As if I know about computers! And then he started to poke around the office and all my folders.

Mr Heath Well he has his job to do, and you can't object to that. What about that other problem you're having putting the figures in?

Sarah   That was partly my fault. I didn't realize that the computer
was supposed to take over all the calculations and records,
and I remember agreeing to that. If I'd realized what it
meant for me I would have said something at the time.
By the way, I still do keep some manual records. The
computer takes two and a half hours to do the sorting on
a Friday.

Mr Heath Yes, that was the other problem. It shouldn't take so long.

Sarah   It doesn't even need to sort. I told him that, but he didn't
want to change the procedures. He ignored some of my ideas.

Mr Heath Well try telling this new wizard everything you can think of,
and don't miss out anything important.

Apart from difficulties with project management some of the
problems are:

> failure to agree objectives,
> failure to ask questions,
> failure to be specific,
> forgetting answers,
> ignoring suggestions,
> making false assumptions,
> failure to explain the consequences of a decision, and
> misunderstanding of terms/jargon.

There are, perhaps, other mistakes here too. Although this
scenario is rather pessimistic and also subjective it shows
clearly how a little carelessness can easily lead to one or more
serious mistakes.

Expert system development

Inasmuch as expert systems are programs, it should come
as little surprise that knowledge elicitation is similar to
systems analysis. By altering our view of the computer user
this analogy should become clearer. Technologists tend to
think of people who are not experts in computer technology
as if they were naïve. In fact, if they are proficient at their
job, they are expert at something, however mundane.

From the programmer's viewpoint a clerk is naïve in
computing, but an expert in his clerical duties; similarly,
the programmer is an expert in some aspects of computing
and naïve with regard to the clerical tasks. It is the systems
analyst's job to ensure that all the necessary details are
extracted from each area in order to produce a computerized
system which carries out functions correctly. Sometimes

the systems analysis is carried out by a programmer; however, this does not invalidate the argument.

In expert systems the expert is more easily identified. He will be recognized by his colleagues as an 'expert', having a body of knowledge which he knows how to apply. Often he will know little about computing, and probably even less about AI. The computer expert will know about computer technology, but very little about the expert's domain. So we have the same situation again. Somehow we must bridge the gap. One way is to use a *knowledge engineer*, analogous to the systems analyst. Once again, the problem is to code in a program all the expertise of the expert so that the program can behave like that expert in tackling certain types of problems. Figure 3.1 shows the analogy between computer systems development and expert systems development.

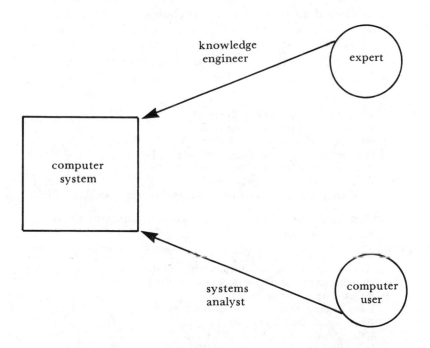

Figure 3.1 *A systems analyst helps a user design computer systems which carry out specific procedures; a knowledge engineer helps design systems which incorporate knowledge from an expert.*

The stages in expert systems development (Hayes-Roth, Waterman & Lenat 1983) can be identified as below (note the similarity with ordinary computer systems development):

Identification — Some task or tasks performed by a human expert is selected as being suitable for an expert system. It is necessary to define the objectives of the expert system: what will it be expected to do? These tasks must be reasonable in terms of available hardware and software facilities. Certain definitions may be relatively vague at this stage, since applications vary so much that almost every project is innovative in some respects. If the project subsequently turns out to be unmanageable then the initial objectives may have to be re-assessed.

Knowledge acquisition — The expert's knowledge has to be extracted and represented in some form so that he can survey the resulting *conceptual model.* This model will very much depend on the domain being studied. As the expert is not explicitly aware of such concepts this stage can involve many hours of discussion and argument. First of all the knowledge engineer and expert must agree on some conceptualization of the problem. This includes issues such as:

What are the inputs or problems?
What are the outputs or solutions?
Which types of inputs cause difficulties for the expert?
How are the problems characterized?
How are the solutions characterized?
What sort of knowledge is used?
How are problems or methods broken down into smaller units?

A later, more detailed, breakdown would answer detailed questions such as:

What data are input; in what order and form?
What are the interrelationships between data items?
How important and how accurate are the data items?
Which data might be missing?
What assumptions does the expert make?
What constraints does he have?
What sort of inferences does he make?
How does he form concepts and hypotheses?
How do these relate to each other?
How does the expert move from one state of belief to another?
Which evidence suggests particular goals or concepts?
What are the causal relationships?

Are there any logical constraints on the system?
Which problems are easy, common, hard, interesting, etc?

Design — Once the conceptual model has been produced, the problem of how this model can be implemented is dealt with. This involves choosing appropriate structures to represent the knowledge base and inference mechanism as they will appear within the expert system.

Development and testing — The design details are then implemented. All aspects of the system have to be tested. Testing can be very difficult, and evaluation is likely to continue well into the early life of the system. Complete testing is extremely difficult for larger systems. It is the very size of some of the problems which actually makes testing difficult. For example, a system comprising 400 rules is far more complex than 'four times a 100 rule system'.

Use — The expert system can then be used, cautiously at first. However, it may be under continuous review and evaluation for some time before it is used with confidence.

These stages are less well-defined than in ordinary computer systems development, and a feasibility study is not generally practicable. Consequently, it might be necessary to review objectives at any stage during development if tasks become more complex than was originally anticipated. Furthermore, the stages overlap a great deal, and it is very difficult to estimate how long each stage might take to complete. Figure 3.2 shows the similarities between systems analysis and knowledge engineering.

Knowledge elicitation — a more difficult problem
The most common methods of fact-finding in systems analysis are: observation and sampling from existing records, interviews or group discussions, and questionnaires or forms. All these are available for knowledge elicitation (Welbank 1983) although, as we shall see, there is a need for more methods.

Systems analysis is a much simpler activity than knowledge elicitation. In systems analysis it is fairly clear what information is required. Questions have to be asked about why, how, how many, how often, when, size, growth,

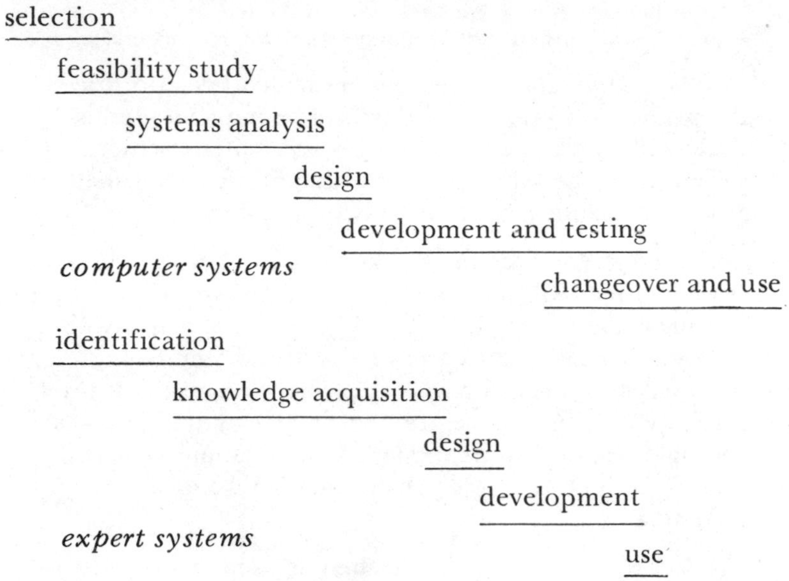

selection

feasibility study

systems analysis

design

development and testing

computer systems

changeover and use

identification

knowledge acquisition

design

development

expert systems

use

Figure 3.2 *Knowledge engineering and systems development —
expert systems are computer-based systems and so the stages in
their development are similar to those in more traditional
computer systems development, although less clearly defined
(note: the diagram is NOT drawn to scale).*

etc. The systems analyst should have a fairly good idea of
what he needs to know. The problems lie in ensuring that he
does not make false assumptions or omissions. This is borne
out by the existence of fairly comprehensive standard forms
to help in recording decisions.

In knowledge acquisition this is not the case. An expert
is not merely someone who knows lots of facts and
procedures. Through years of experience he has built up a
body of knowledge which he uses to make informed and wise
decisions. Some of his knowledge has come about through his
particular experiences, and cannot be found in a text book or
set of procedural rules. He often makes judgements based on
intuition. It is more than likely that he has never had to state
explicitly how he makes these judgements and decisions. The
knowledge engineer's routine is therefore much less well
defined; hence, a whole new set of difficulties exist in
knowledge acquisition.

Summary

An expert system is a program, or set of programs. The process of building such a system is therefore similar to that of 'traditional' computer systems development. There are various similarities between the two processes and much to be learnt from the existing documentation on systems analysis. However, the fact that we are dealing with knowledge rather than procedures makes knowledge acquisition much more complex and difficult.

CHAPTER 4

The knowledge engineer

In computer systems development the systems analyst plays
a key role in the planning and management of a project.
Systems analysts are skilled people with good technical and
inter-personal skills. The success of a project can depend to a
large extent on the analysts and the system designers. This
chapter explores some of the problems in expert systems
development, and examines the role played by knowledge
engineers, particularly in the early stages of development.

The role of the systems analyst
We have already described the stages of development of a
computer-based system, and some of the likely problems
have been indicated. Computers are used to solve problems,
and meet defined objectives within an organization. The users
of the system usually know little about the technical details
of hardware and software. On the other hand, the computer
programmers will not know a great deal about the specific
problems and demands of all users. If a computer system is to
meet requirements in a satisfactory way, given the constraints
of time and cost, then the two bodies of knowledge must be
married together.

Although users have a very important input to the analysis
and design of such systems, they cannot operate without help
and guidance. The person guiding them needs sound technical
knowledge, good communication skills, and the right personal
qualities to be able to minimize any hostility, fear or
reluctance on the part of the users. Some organizations
employ systems analysts for this work, but nowadays some
programmers help with systems analysis and design. What is
clear is that technical knowledge is not sufficient in itself;
users must believe that the project is worthwhile, that they

can make a useful contribution to its development, and that they can work effectively with the analysis team.

The role of the knowledge engineer

We have described some of the ways in which knowledge elicitation is more complex than systems analysis, and how the knowledge engineer is analogous to the systems analyst. There are, therefore, two main reasons why an expert should not be his own knowledge engineer:

- he will usually have insufficient knowledge about programming and expert system techniques, and
- he will find it difficult to describe his knowledge completely and correctly.

However, the programmer could act as the knowledge engineer provided he has the right inter-personal skills (Feigenbaum & McCorduck 1984; Welbank 1983). Some of these are described below:

Good communication skills — The knowledge elicitation will involve many hours of discussion and argument. Results have to be recorded, and conclusions or models agreed with the expert. This necessitates the effective use of the spoken and written word, diagrammatic representation, and interpretation of body language. Above all there must be a good relationship between the knowledge engineer and expert. A poor communicator cannot make a good knowledge engineer.

Intelligence — The knowledge engineer is continually learning. As he starts a new project he needs to be able to learn about a new knowledge domain, and understand enough of the terminology and principles to be able to discuss it fully with an acknowledged expert. He must keep up-to-date with advances in hardware and software. In addition, he needs to have a knowledge of subjects such as formal logic, probability theory and psychology, and be able to appreciate the relevance of developments in these subjects. He needs to keep an open mind and be able to tackle problems in different ways.

Tact and diplomacy — The success of the project will depend on the cooperation of a small number (often one) of important experts. An expert who has been alienated by thoughtless or tactless treatment will tend to lose interest. Any suggestion that a program can replace or outperform the expert can be disastrous. So is an intimation that the expert is failing to provide the right information in an appropriate way.

Empathy and patience — The knowledge engineer and expert must work together as a team, each respecting the other. This means that the knowledge engineer must appreciate the problems faced by the expert. He needs to encourage without being patronizing, to argue without appearing self-opinionated, and ask for clarification without appearing critical. If he realizes the reasons for the expert's hesitancy or apparent incoherence then he will be able to exercise sufficient patience.

Persistence — Results may come slowly. Ultimately, there must be no gaps or inconsistencies, but during development there may be many. In order to resolve problems the knowledge engineer must persist; he must retain his enthusiasm and belief in the project. Despite setbacks, he must persist in the conviction that success will come.

Logicality — The inference mechanism of the expert system must be consistent and logical. During knowledge elicitation, especially the early stages, the expert's explanations may seem confused or fragmented. The elicitor needs to be able to argue reasonably, recognizing valid statements and providing meaningful counter-examples for possible errors. The completeness and consistency of the emerging model must also be assessed. All of this requires a level of clear thought and logicality.

Versatility and inventiveness — Until recognized methodologies are developed, or shells are produced with very flexible structures, the methods used to elicit a model of expertise will rely heavily on the knowledge engineer. Using his judgement he will have to select methods which seem appropriate, and abandon those which are not effective. He may have to discard early results or models, and if necessary invent representations which suit the expert and the domain. This requires an informed, versatile approach to the project, together with an ability and willingness to try new ideas.

Self confidence — The combination of these qualities and skills must be matched by self confidence. A shy or immature person, however technically able, would not be able to control a project. The development of an expert system is a challenge, and the knowledge engineer must have enough self confidence to sustain enthusiasm for the project. At the same time this confidence must not result in bombastic or patronizing behaviour.

Domain knowledge — The knowledge engineer has to talk to the expert using the expert's terminology. It would be advantageous, therefore, for the knowledge engineer to have some background knowledge of the domain, for example, the types of problems encountered, the terminology, accepted methods and tools.

Programming knowledge — The knowledge base and inference mechanisms used by the expert will be implemented in a program. It is advisable, but not essential, that the knowledge engineer understands programming and the various forms of knowledge representation available, e.g. semantic nets and frames. However, during knowledge elicitation an intelligent and versatile approach is most important, and some deficiencies in computer science experience can be tolerated.

It is unlikely that a knowledge engineer would have all these qualities, since personnel for a particular project are often sought from existing staff, rather than employing new specialists. This list is included to give an idea of the optimal person's talents and the ways in which they are likely to be needed. However, it is certain that the selection of the knowledge engineer will have a crucial effect on the success of a project. It is useful at this point to explore the tasks required of the knowledge engineer.

PROJECT MANAGEMENT
In Chapter 3 some relatively common problems in systems analysis were described: these problems were associated with the liaison between the analyst and user. Subsequent chapters will be concerned with the detailed extraction of knowledge from experts by a knowledge eliciter. If the project itself is poorly planned or ill-managed then it will most certainly fail, despite the ingenuity of an efficient knowledge engineer.

Typical mistakes in project management (Hayes Roth,
Waterman & Lenat 1983) are:

bad evaluation of project aims and objectives,
bad planning of times and resources,
inappropriate choice of knowledge domain,
imprecise objectives,
insufficient involvement of management,
failure to get agreement of schedule and objectives,
change of key staff during the project,
change of objectives without reassessment of feasibility,
inadequate documentation,
purpose not clear to management or users, and
no targets or checkpoints.

The innovative nature of expert system projects means that
detailed planning of development activities is extremely
difficult. Nevertheless, there is no reason to ignore usual
project guidelines or codes of practice. The project will
necessitate the active and time-consuming involvement of key
personnel, and so objectives and constraints must be
established and agreed on at the start. Management must
understand the nature of the project before authorizing it.
They should also be informed about progress and consulted
about any significant changes or problems. All agreements
must be recorded. The importance of recording all detailed
discussions and results should be stressed. Tentative plans
and estimates of resources should be made, even if they are
accompanied by a written disclaimer. An inadequate plan or
schedule is better than none at all.

In Chapter 3 the stages in the project development and the
areas where they could overlap were outlined. Before
describing any detailed methods of knowledge acquisition
it is necessary to understand the tasks which will feature in
a successful project.

PROJECT IDENTIFICATION
A working and effective expert system will certainly be of
great benefit to an organization. However, its success cannot
be guaranteed, and embarking on a development programme
will involve the allocation of additional people, resources and
money. At the early stages of development it is essential that
the project is considered very carefully. A cost-benefit analysis
might not prove feasible, but the potential benefits of the
proposed investment should be made clear. At this stage the

43

knowledge engineer might not have been identified, but it is desirable to have him involved as early as possible.

Experience has shown (Goodall 1985) that the most successful projects are those with fairly modest objectives, taking about six man-months to develop. The problem should be clearly defined and bounded, i.e. it should be easy to describe what the expert system should do, its use and scope. Furthermore, the chosen problem must be sufficiently important to warrant investigation, while being technically feasible. Questions to be asked include (Hayes Roth, Waterman and Lenat 1983):

How important is this problem?
What would be the advantages of an expert system?
How common is the problem?
How important will it be in a few years' time?
Can the problem be easily defined?
Would it be practical to use a computer?
Has anyone tried a similar project elsewhere?
Who would use the expert system? Why?
Is there a shell we could use?
Is there any documentation?
How do the experts learn their expertise?
Can we spare an expert's time?
What resources do we need?
What might make this project difficult to develop?
Do the experts disagree?
How long does it take to become an expert?
How much can be invested in this project?
Are there any times when the experts are not available for consultation?
Is the knowledge complex, needing several inferences mechanisms and knowledge representations?
Will the expert system need updating frequently?
Can we tolerate imperfect output?
Will the development of the interface require great effort?

A discussion along these lines will help to identify possible difficulties, to reach agreement on sensible objectives, and to draw up plans for the development of a project having obvious commercial benefits. We can illustrate some of these points by considering this description of the rationale behind a project to develop an expert computer-aided design (CAD) system.

'At the start lots of us were a bit wary about artificial intelligence. It all sounded a bit like science fiction. So we read up about what other people had done. That took some of the magic out of it, and it seemed like a good move in CAD.

CAD covers lots of things, and computers are used already. But there's lots of scope for mistakes by designers. We thought maybe we could get rid of some of those mistakes. But we didn't want the computer to take over. We wanted it to help the designer, and take the responsibility for some of the routine (but clever) stuff. He would keep the creativity. So we had to think of a product, and what we could use.

There was no chance of another computer, and a lot of our routines were in FORTRAN, so we thought we'd better do it in something on our machine which would interface with our FORTRAN routines. Also we couldn't afford to get anyone else in, so one of the programmers would have to do the knowledge acquisition. That tied us down a bit.

It seemed obvious that we had to decide on the particular product and write our expert adviser for that. It could be extended if it was any good. We chose widgets. At the moment we don't make too many, but we're going to. They're not too hard but mistakes are costly. There are lots of rules to be remembered — not all of them written down. You sometimes forget them. The two people we've got off them have their own method — they developed it together. They say it isn't too hard, but other people can't do it. One of these people could spare a fair amount of time over the following four months, and the other one wouldn't mind chipping in. Also, the programmer knew a bit about it already, so that seemed like the best project.'

Many of the questions have been answered qualitatively if not quantitatively. For this venture management and experts had established what they were doing and why, and attempted to solve a modest problem before tackling really complex ones.

Once the project has been defined and authorized the knowledge engineer starts his preparatory work (Feigenbaum & McCorduck 1984; Welbank 1983). There are various aspects to this background research.

Understanding the problem — Although the problem may have been defined, the knowledge engineer might still need further information. By talking to people or monitoring departments at work he can familiarize himself with the daily operations of the staff. He should glean as much information as possible before contacting the experts, so that he can understand what the expert does, and where this particular aspect fits into the whole problem.

Background reading — There will usually be text books or manuals relating to the subject area. These should be studied. They will not often describe an expert's knowledge, but they are a good source for general terms of reference,

45

definition of terms peculiar to the subject area, and descriptions of routine or common procedures.

Existing documentation — In addition to published material there may be in-house case histories or documents. These can give information about cases dealt with by a specific department, and indicate common, or difficult cases.

Location of experts — If the experts have not been identified then they must be named. Before approaching any of them the knowledge engineer must make sure that he at least knows their name, responsibility, position and job. He should also know who needs to contact the expert, when he can be seen, and how much the expert already knows about the project.

In short, the knowledge engineer should do as much as he possibly can to find out about the chosen knowledge domain before trying to talk with an expert. He must also ensure that the expert fully understands the relevance of their meeting.

KNOWLEDGE ACQUISITION
The task of knowledge elicitation can now begin in earnest. The processes of eliciting, designing and implementing can overlap during project development, so knowledge acquisition pervades all the stages. Perhaps the most important objective of project control is to retain the willing involvement of the expert.

Problems can arise if the expert cancels or defers appointments, fails to answer questions, or neglects to supply information. The knowledge engineer has to assess why this is happening, and how it can be corrected. Experts are busy and often not available for consultation for long periods of time. Even an enthusiastic expert may be unavailable for days or weeks; at worst he may lose interest and deliberately make himself unavailable. A more difficult problem arises if the expert develops a subconscious hostility or fear. This will mean that he fails to provide the correct information even when he is seeming to cooperate. There is no easy solution to such problems, though the knowledge engineer should seek to maintain a good personal relationship with the expert at an early stage of project development so that he can make reasonable judgements about his behaviour later on. An error of judgement on why an expert is failing to cooperate can result in a very serious problem.

Another problem which can occur is that the expert might, consciously or subconsciously, use the knowledge engineer — if he finds the process of knowledge elicitation interesting, or he is keen to understand his own knowledge — to experiment with different models of his knowledge domain that he has developed. This will always be time consuming, possibly useful, but generally experimentation without the eliciter being aware of it is confusing and usually hinders progress.

Most of the problems are caused by the fact that the process of knowledge elicitation requires many hours of an expert who is already busy and has many demands on his time. This is best illustrated by some quotes from knowledge engineers:

'When I tried to make appointments to see him, he tried to divert me to the other person. I specially wanted him, because he's more likely to tell me the truth. The other one would only give me the text book version. In the end I did get him. Then he behaved quite differently depending whether the tape recorder was on or off. He was a bit cautious when the recorder was on. After I switched it off he really started telling me what I wanted. I daren't switch it back on. I just tried to remember it all and scribbled it down as soon as I got out of the room.'

'I didn't always understand what he was saying. I had a technician there who did. But when we came to play back the recordings it was very hard. When we were in the room with him we knew what he was talking about. On the tape we couldn't see him waving his hands, and it wasn't clear whether he was smiling or frowning. Out of context a lot of it was just rubbish.'

'At first he swore blind that it was impossible. I decided not to press him. So I told him where the machine was, and left the manual by it. He'd said he was too busy. He got hooked. I came in early one morning and found him using the program. At first he didn't want me to see. It was amazing. He'd built a fantastically complicated network. After that we couldn't get him off it, and now he won't let us have it until he's got it 'perfect'.'

'I thought he was being awkward. His answers were either trite or not at all. He's an eloquent man. He was a wreck. After asking the same question too many times I decided to leave him alone. I asked him to try to draw it out. It was a gamble, but after a couple of weeks he rang me up to say he'd got something. He had.'

Comments from experts are less readily available; however, some do make remarks . . .

'He kept interrupting me and asking the same question. I found it almost impossible at first because we didn't speak the same language.'

'Initially I believed it was stupid. Then I started to write it down. "This is just like an adventure game", I thought. It appeared simplistic and superficial, but apparently it was what he wanted.'

'I did not know what he wanted. I was quite happy to help, and keen to see the program working, but I kept asking myself what I should be doing. He didn't say much, but just watched. When I got some feedback — a trifle late — I started to understand.'

Unfortunately, few researchers formally report problems with the expert, and the best way to appreciate them is to talk to people who are prepared to discuss their experiences.

Summary
The knowledge engineer is a key person in the project development. The selection of a suitably qualified person is important because he must establish the right sort of relationship with the expert and maintain it throughout the project. The knowledge engineer must ensure that the project is approached and managed sensibly, and that the work carried out is worthwhile.

CHAPTER 5

Fact-finding by interviews

A systems analyst can fact-find by questionnaire, by sampling records or by observing people at work, but no analysis is complete without face-to-face discussions with users. In fact the current philosophy is that users should be actively involved at the systems design stage, as well as at the analysis stage. Now that there are established methodologies for systems analysis, the problems associated with the communication of ideas during fact-finding have, to a large extent, been overcome. Users and analysts should be able to work together to produce systems which are technically feasible and of practical benefit. As has already been said, a user can seldom design systems by himself and, in the same way, it is usually the case that the expert does not also act as the knowledge engineer.

There will, therefore, be several meetings or discussions between the knowledge engineer and domain expert, as between analyst and user. Ideally these sessions should be planned; the knowledge engineer should have specific objectives and questions in mind. Unfortunately, owing to the very nature of expertise, no methodology has been established for this and interviews are likely to become ill structured, and the information gained can be incomplete and inadequate. As with systems analysis, communication skills and inter-personal skills are of great importance in the development of effective expert systems.

General principles
The approach of the knowledge engineer will depend on the particular expert and the knowledge domain (Welbank 1983), but the following guidelines might be appropriate.

Be specific, not general — The expert may not have remembered rules or concepts, and so he will find it difficult to recall them. He will find it easier to talk about specific, interesting or unusual cases. He may find it easier to apply methods rather than to describe them. So instead of asking very general questions the knowledge engineer should encourage the expert to describe particular problems which are of interest, or which are readily available to him. This can be crucially important in the early stages of systems development.

Do not impose alien tools — The expert should be encouraged to provide the information in a way which is most natural to him. This means making maximum use of graphs, tables, diagrams, etc which often are already available. The expert should not be forced to produce a representation (e.g. a flowchart) which he would not normally use. Even doodles or scribbles on a piece of paper can be useful. If the expert uses a representation which he finds natural and easy then the information contained in it is less likely to be corrupted or distorted, and will represent more accurately the expert's actual thought processes. The knowledge engineer can always ask for clarification or amplification if he does not fully understand the representation used.

Do not interrupt — The aim is to get the expert talking. Despite the fact that the expert will probably digress or repeat himself, interruptions should be kept to a minimum. The knowledge engineer should be patient, and expect contradictions and inconsistencies. This can be very trying, and requires discipline on the part of the knowledge engineer. However, implied criticism or interruptions can prevent the expert from providing useful, or even vital, information. The knowledge engineer can seldom judge what is most relevant in the dialogue at the time, and might not know where the expert's train of thought is leading. Unless he is absolutely sure that the expert has digressed completely, he should still listen carefully. Learning to observe the expert's body language and sense when he is hesitant or confused can help the engineer to make helpful interruptions when this is appropriate.

Record information — Even if the questions have been

planned, it is not always clear which parts of the dialogue are most important. A throw-away remark can turn out to be fundamentally important. Very often interviews are tape-recorded and later transcribed. The expert will become annoyed if he needs to keep repeating information. If interviews are not tape-recorded then all information should be written down as soon as possible after the event, while it is fresh in the knowledge engineer's mind. The methodical recording and cross-referencing of material can be a key factor in the success of elicitation and subsequent design. This can be a complicated task, but until there are well-tested methods the eliciter cannot afford to dispose or lose track of any elicited knowledge.

An alternative method to tape-recording is to video-record interviews. This has the distinct advantage of recording body language as well as speech, and thereby enables comments to be interpreted in context. However, some people find the presence of a camera inhibiting. Although some knowledge engineers have played back recordings to the expert and asked for comments, some people find this disconcerting also.

Above all, the expert must be in an environment which he finds conducive to easy dialogue. The knowledge engineer must have regard for the expert's feelings and not use a method which causes stress or feels intrusive.

Listen to the way the expert uses knowledge — It is not just the facts, theories and heuristics which are important. The eliciter should listen carefully to the way in which the expert manipulates his knowledge. This will not be stated explicitly, and once the eliciter has theories about this implicit content he must discuss them with the expert. These include points such as the order in which he approaches problems, the relative importance attached to different items, and the ways in which he weighs evidence. Some of these observations might be new to the expert, and the eliciter needs to take care not to make theories which are based on tenuous evidence or optimistic guesswork. He should also exercise patience as the expert considers new theories or speculates about his work. Hypotheses based on a single statement are to be viewed sceptically. On the other hand, where there is apparent

51

duplication of rules or information the knowledge engineer might be able to detect a general principle or concept.

Objectives

What is required from the elicitation stage is a complete and correct description of the expert's knowledge, and the way in which he handles that knowledge, in the specific area of expertise which is being investigated. The actual details of what is involved in this depend very much on the knowledge domain, so no definitive description can be given. At a simplistic level the knowledge can be regarded as facts and rules, but in practice this is far too simplistic; as has already been said, knowledge is more complex, involving intermediate states of belief, conjectures and assumptions. It is the way in which the expert handles and manipulates the knowledge which is important; in particular, the way he deals with incompleteness and uncertainty.

Systems analysis and systems design are distinct activities. The practical constraints of what can be implemented on available hardware and software should not be an overriding influence on systems analysis. In the same way, knowledge representation is different from knowledge elicitation. However, the knowledge engineer is almost bound to anticipate how a particular inference method or knowledge base can be represented, and tailor questions accordingly. So the objectives of questioning depend on both the knowledge domain and the possible representation. At this stage in research and development it is difficult to be more specific; we are not sure about the cognitive processes used in decision-making, and a method that is most appropriate for a particular project must be used.

It is possible to give some simple examples. Figure 5.1 shows a tabular representation of knowledge where facts, definitions, assumptions, answers to questions, rules and decisions have been identified as the key elements. In this case the rules describe how the inputs are used to obtain the output decisions.

Figure 5.2 shows an alternative approach. Here the expert has produced a table summarizing the different classes of problem he encounters. Each case is described by its characteristics and the ensuing decision. The rules are implicit in the table, and not explicitly stated, and need to be clarified

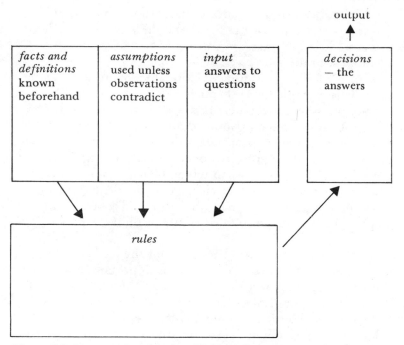

output

facts and definitions known beforehand	assumptions used unless observations contradict	input answers to questions		decisions — the answers

rules

Figure 5.1 *Data consist of facts which are always true, and assumptions which are normally true. Answers that are input can override assumptions. The rules combine all the data to give a resulting decision. The knowledge is displayed in lists and rules.*

characteristics			decision	
size	colour	age	depth	class
large	red	10	24.8	I
small	red	12	30.3	I
—	—	—	—	—
—	—	—	—	—
—	—	—	—	—
small	black	18	12.7	II
large	black	14	11.3	II
large	black	15	50.4	III
small	red	17	47.3	III
—	—	—	—	—
—	—	—	—	—
—	—	—	—	—

Figure 5.2 *The expert draws up a table of different classes of problem which he meets. Each case is described by its characteristics and the ensuing decision. The rules are implicit in the table, and are not explicitly stated.*

with the expert. (If appropriate, induction can be used here; this is described in Chapter 8.) It should be noted that in this case the expert has agreed on a subset of terms which can appear in the table.

Figure 5.3 illustrates how existing documentation can be used. This example arose through an exercise on weather prediction, where the expert had a set of seven graphs. The expertise lay in matching input data to one of these seven graphs, and making appropriate recommendations. Once the importance of the graphs had been agreed, the expert talked quite freely about the way in which he used them. At first he had been reticent about describing his knowledge and an alert knowledge engineer had observed, and asked about, the graphs which he saw displayed on the wall of the expert's office.

This example illustrates the fact that the environment in which the interview is conducted is important, and that the knowledge engineer should make use of existing documents, reports, files, etc.

Figure 5.4 shows an *inference network* with attributes and rules. These diagrams are very versatile and can quite often be useful; however, they can become complicated and untidy. Attributes are the data, i.e. observations, facts, etc. which form the preconditions to some rules and the targets for others. For example rule 4 (R4) is of the form IF A3 AND A6 THEN A8.

Figure 5.5 shows a *decision tree* structure with elaborations and added comments. A decision tree is similar to a flow chart, but consists of nodes and branches. Terminal nodes are those at the bottom, and the others are intermediate nodes. In this case, we branch down the tree along a path depending on the value of an attribute described in an intermediate node until a terminal node (the decision) is reached. The left side of the tree reads: 'If rainfall is high and temperature is low and sunshine is less than four hours, then it will rain tomorrow; if rainfall is high and temperature is low and sunshine is greater than four hours, then it will not rain tomorrow.'

The expert and knowledge engineer need to agree on a representation which is mutually acceptable and useful. The choice may change as the project gets under way and neither party should be unwilling to 'start again'. However,

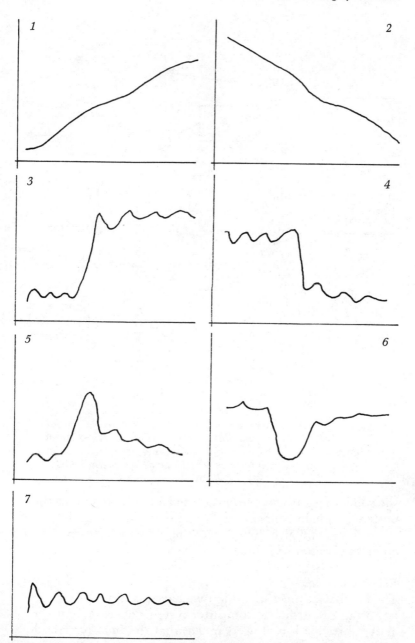

Figure 5.3 *The expert's skill lies in matching input data to one of the seven graphs shown above and then making appropriate weather predictions. In this case knowledge elicitation centres on these graphs.*

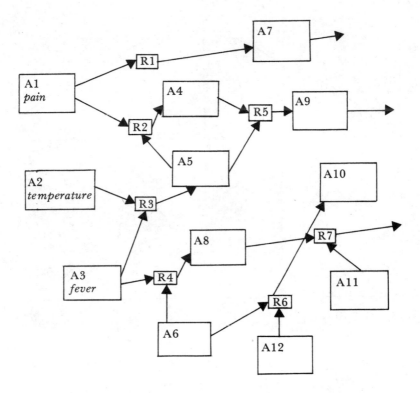

Figure 5.4 *An inference network is a versatile tool, but diagrams can get complicated. Here the boxes represent attributes or states, and rules. The diagram shows how the rules relate to the attributes, and indicates how inference is built up across the network.*

the sooner results can be represented and documented, the better. This helps the expert to maintain interest and enthusiasm, and gives him something on which he can comment or modify.

Feedback

The feedback aspect, to which we have just referred, is very important. In ordinary computer systems development the active participation of users means that the final systems are acceptable and useful to a company or establishment as a whole, and not just to the computer experts. The education and training of users starts at the very early stages of

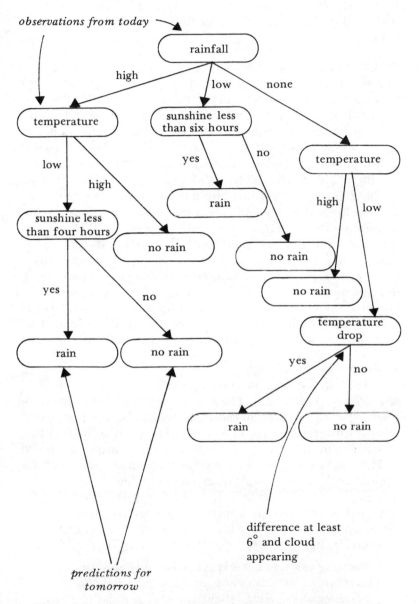

Figure 5.5 *A decision tree: we branch down the tree along a path
depending on the value of the attributes. At the end of a path
we find the prediction of weather for the next day
depending on the observed characteristics of today's weather.*

development as users learn about what computers can do and how they can be used in systems. The general enthusiasm sustained in this approach results in systems of greater overall benefit.

INTERMEDIATE RESULTS
In knowledge elicitation the development team has to believe in the merits of a project and the value of the intermediate results. Both the expert and eliciter are learning about what is possible and what is valuable. For the expert to maintain his enthusiasm and willing cooperation, he should be able to see that his effort is productive. This means that early on he should be able to discuss tentative results or models. Even if he disagrees with the model, he should be able to make constructive criticism, and this is usually an excellent method of eliciting further facts, rules and explanations. Whereas the expert might forget important information during questioning, he will find it far easier to criticize or evaluate a formulation presented to him. Intermediate results are an indication that the hours of questioning and discussion with a knowledge engineer are producing something of value. They also encourage the knowledge engineer to record and analyse findings, and sustain *his* enthusiasm for the project.

Methods of questioning

There are methods of questioning that are recognized in psychology (Puff 1982). The knowledge engineer needs to be aware of each of these methods, and must use them as and when appropriate. A method which seems not to be fruitful should not be pursued when another might be more successful.

The aim is to obtain information from the expert, and the eliciter's role is to prompt, question, help, and suggest inconsistencies or counter-examples. Best results will be obtained when the expert and eliciter work together as a team, using a method which both find helpful. Typical methods include:

Interesting cases — The expert is asked to describe interesting or difficult cases which he can recall, and his experience and feelings at the time. This is called the *critical incident technique.* By describing his feelings the expert is more likely to give an accurate account of what he was doing. Difficult or interesting cases are more

memorable and stimulating. The expert may omit essential
details about mundane or easy cases, but this specific
form of questioning can give very useful information
quickly and form the basis for further discussion. However,
the eliciter should take care that he does not mistake
interesting cases for common or typical ones. The expert
himself may have a biased view of what is representative.
This will need to be resolved later.

Characteristics and decisions — While unable to formulate
rules or heuristics, the expert may be able to give lists of
symptoms or characteristics, and possible decisions. Given
these, the expert can then be asked to match sets of
charactcristics to decisions. In this approach the rules
are *implicit* rather than explicit, and the expert is not
constrained by having to speculate about the rules which
he thinks he might use. Some people find this surprisingly
easy once they have started. On the other hand some
experts find this an artificial situation since it does not
include the order in which symptoms are encountered in
real life.

Distinguishing goals — Goals (intermediate or final) are
states of belief, or decisions. Given a specific goal the
expert can be asked to specify the sets of evidence which
are necessary and sufficient to distinguish this goal from
the other alternatives. If he does this for the final goal, and
then for each of the intermediate goals, he can build up a
structured model of his knowledge. This method provokes
discussion about the precise nature of and reasons for the
goals.

Reclassification — The expert may find it easier to work
backwards from a goal rather than forwards from a set of
symptoms. Each goal can be reclassified into evidences for
that goal. These may be specific and observable, or general.
The general sub-goals are successively reclassified until the
evidence has been broken down into observable symptoms
or facts.

Dividing the domain — This is similar to reclassification,
but works in reverse. Instead of starting with goals the
expert starts by describing symptoms, and successively
groups them until he reaches the final goal.

Talk-through — Instead of asking the expert to describe
what he has done or to imagine what he would do, he can
be asked to think aloud while at work. In this way he talks
through a specific case, and the comments can then be
captured. This talk-through should be tape-recorded and a
protocol typed from the transcript. The case can be real
and unseen, existing and documented, or hypothetical.
If decisions are usually made under time pressure then a
simulation can give the opportunity for the expert to
describe details, stopping at the stages of greatest interest
or difficulty.

Decision analysis — Methods of decision analysis have been
applied in many areas of management and business. The
general method is:

1) List all possible decisions.
2) For each decision list the possible consequences.
3) For each consequence assess its worth and the
   probability of its occurrence.
4) Calculate the expected worth of each consequence
   by multiplying worth by probability.
5) Calculate the expected worth of a decision as the
   total of all the expected worths of its consequences.
6) Select the decision which maximizes the expected
   worth.

While this method is intuitively appealing it has the
fundamental problem that it relies on estimates of worth
and probability (Johnson-Laird & Wason 1977; Scholz
1983). However, in certain instances the expert might be
happy to evaluate his decision-making in this way. The
problems of dealing with probability are discussed in full
in Chapter 6.

Analysis

Once the transcipts or recorded answers have been produced
they have to be analysed and refined until the knowledge is
in a suitable format to meet the general objectives. This
requires great skill, and it is difficult to ensure consistency
and lack of redundancy in the results. There are some
techniques which can be of help.

In general, diagrams are easier to analyse than directly

reported speech, although their information content may be lower. Natural speech is marked by part-sentences, contradictions, omissions and repetitions. Body language and other inaudible events or stimuli will not be recorded. Remarks may be difficult to understand after the event, and out of context. The use of words is often inconsistent and imprecise.

During analysis the raw information is refined, edited and re-organized. The original should always be retained, and labelled with the details of the interview, i.e. purpose, date, name of expert, etc. It is also a good idea to number lines in a transcript. Subsequent modifications should be cross-referenced back to these originals. Some amount of knowledge can be extracted directly: facts, assumptions and rules may be stated explicitly, albeit in context. These have to be extracted from the other seemingly irrelevant details, co-ordinated, and structured. The knowledge engineer has also to infer the implicit knowledge which the expert is using. This may be background knowledge, evidence which is not recorded, or the identification of referents like 'it' and 'that' (see Newell & Simon 1972). The order of analysis or reasoning has to be extracted too. Certain answers trigger further questions, or back-tracking: this is all part of the expert's inference procedure.

Systems analysts use a data dictionary to record significant findings during analysis (Gane & Sarson 1979). A data dictionary is used to define any terms referred to during the analysis. It describes items and the relationships between them. Similarly, a *knowledge dictionary*, i.e. a systematic catalogue of items of interest, can be drawn up, either on a database or in a manual system. Typical contents of such a dictionary might be:

    name
    type (fact, goal, evidence, etc.)
    aliases — synonyms or alternative names
    attributes or characteristics
    possible values
    importance
    prior belief/assumption if uncertain evidence
    evidence required — prerequisites
    rules triggered or goals considered
    cross-reference to source in elicitation
    special comments about use/implications

Word processors can be useful in analysing verbal reports, and special tools based on word processors (knowledge processors) are under development. These enable dictionaries to be set up, chunks of text to be moved around, and facilitate cross-referencing. Alternatively, at a much lower level highlighting pens and notes in the margin of the transcript can be used to extract and structure material.

A well-designed database removes many of the problems of inconsistency, duplication and redundancy of data which can arise in multi-file designs. For example, in a multi-file system the same data item can appear several times and this causes problems when updating and deleting data. In order to achieve a good design, the data have to be arranged into a sensible and optimal structure. This involves asking questions about which data items are directly related to each other, and which indirectly, and organizing the data into 'natural' aggregates. Similar principles can be applied to knowledge analysis in an attempt to structure knowledge. As yet these methods have not been formalized, but in an attempt to structure it knowledge should be classified as basic elements, classes and sets, relationships, inputs, strategies, knowledge states, goals, etc. A knowledge dictionary can form the basis for this. The first stage of analysis is to identify the knowledge elements and the relationships between them. The second stage is to describe the ways in which the elements are used by the expert; this is sometimes called *functional analysis.*

EXAMPLES OF ANALYSIS
The following extracts from interviews illustrate three different approaches:

Reclassification — An examiner describing how he makes judgements about student performance.

'. . . I can do one of three things — pass, fail or refer. Or there are special cases which don't really fall into these categories, but they're rare. Perhaps they do actually fall into one of these three. Yes, they do, because these are the only possible decisions: sometimes we just bend the rules a bit if there's a good reason.

Passing is relatively easy. They pass if they've met all the requirements. That means exams and assessments. If they pass everything there's nothing to argue about. Sometimes they're allowed to pass if they've gone down a bit in one subject. This would be a marginal failure, and there would be evidence of strengths in the subject elsewhere. I can give more details about these sorts.

Students are referred if they should have passed, but didn't. If we thought they would have done well. They fluff it — and not marginally. So we think they're really worthy of a pass, and we give them a second chance to prove that they deserve it. So the mark would be above 30%. Not too many subjects. It depends, there may be extenuating circumstances. We do argue about these . . .'

Figure 5.6 shows the structure for this approach. As he proceeds, the expert slowly gives more details about the types of cases which fall into each of the classes.

Dividing the domain — an admissions tutor describing how he deals with applications to a course.

'. . . Now, we get applications from different backgrounds. They're all quite different. Experience tells you this. My decisions are based on my experience and seeing how well they do on the course.

Mature students are completely different. They can break all the rules. I'll tell you about those later.

Students from background A — they wouldn't be mature — they're usually OK. This is a good basis for the course. Everybody says so. You see they have the requirements, and they're quite bright . . . Of course you have to check the reference. If it's fishy you begin to get suspicious. Usually it isn't. Look at the form as well. Is it filled in right? It depends whether you're looking for reasons to reject. I don't often reject these . . .

From background B they're different. They haven't done much maths. Look at the form. It won't be filled in very well. Messy. Have you seen any? Look at this one . . . it's not very good. They aren't. If they impress you then look carefully. Scrutinize the form. They could be good, but that would be unusual . . .'

Figure 5.7 shows a representation for this method. This time the expert is describing the types of cases he encounters and how he classifies them.

Talk-through — a transcript of a wood-carver describing a piece of wood.

'. . . No two pieces of wood look the same. Hmm . . . This is a nice plate. It looks brown — dark. See here underneath it's stained. The wood is light coloured underneath. See . . . That's why you have to be careful. It looks yellow. Yes, yellow, not brown. The brown isn't . . . It's quite clear.

It's very light. Light and yellow. I mean no weight.

Probably pine. They often use pine for decorative plates. It's very easy to carve.

Pine would be two-coloured. Yes. Here, see. Dark and light — clear. You don't get pores with pine. It's soft I can . . . with a nail — see. No, there aren't any pores . . .'

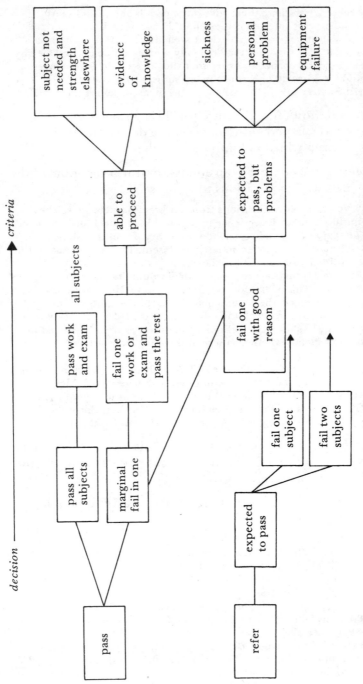

Figure 5.6 *Reclassification: the expert starts with the decision and works towards the different examples for that decision; as he works across then the information becomes detailed.*

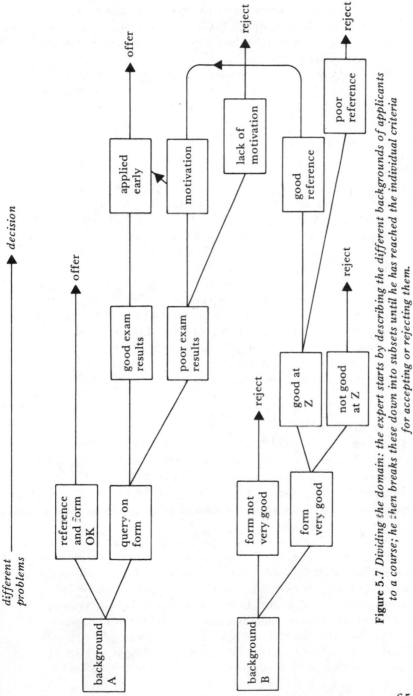

Figure 5.7 *Dividing the domain: the expert starts by describing the different backgrounds of applicants to a course; he then breaks these down into subsets until he has reached the individual criteria for accepting or rejecting them.*

From this simple example we can extract facts, e.g. pine wood does not have pores; a list of characteristics of wood, e.g. colours, pores, weight, hardness; and the way in which the expert analyses this particular example.

To obtain more general results further protocols should be analysed in order to establish the way in which problems are approached. It would also be necessary to obtain descriptions of the characteristics of different woods and their uses (Figure 5.8 illustrates this method).

Protocol analysis

The analysis of these protocols can be a long and tedious task, but it has proved useful in several projects. First of all it is necessary to identify phrases with a high information content, and then to group these phrases into areas of knowledge (Newell & Simon 1972). Once these areas have been defined it is necessary to show the interrelationship between them, and the criteria for passing from one area, or state of belief, to another. It is very important to represent group rules and concepts rather than to adopt a piecemeal approach. Wherever possible an attempt should be made to structure results. As the model is being developed it is advisable to 'freeze' it and to test it before further refinement. Once again, a knowledge dictionary can form the basis of this analysis.

Other methods

So far we have implicitly assumed that there is only one expert. The presence of more experts does not make a great difference to the questioning techniques, but experts can disagree. If there is more than one expert in the project then each item of knowledge should be labelled with its source, i.e. the expert's name.

An alternative strategy is to put all the experts in a room and let them argue out a formulation of the expertise. This works particularly well if there are disagreements which are sufficient to provoke discussion but not severe enough to preclude any agreement. It will probably still be necessary to record the discussions, because the final model may make many assumptions about background knowledge. Often the expense of releasing several experts for lengthy periods of time prohibits such an approach. A cheaper method is for

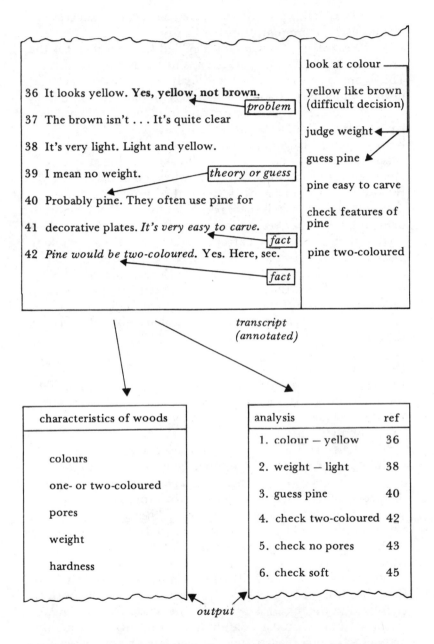

36 It looks yellow. **Yes, yellow, not brown.** ⟵ *problem*

37 The brown isn't . . . It's quite clear

38 It's very light. Light and yellow.

39 I mean no weight.

40 Probably pine. They often use pine for ⟵ *theory or guess*

41 decorative plates. *It's very easy to carve.* ⟵ *fact*

42 *Pine would be two-coloured.* Yes. Here, see. ⟵ *fact*

look at colour

yellow like brown
(difficult decision)

judge weight

guess pine

pine easy to carve

check features of
pine

pine two-coloured

*transcript
(annotated)*

characteristics of woods

colours

one- or two-coloured

pores

weight

hardness

analysis	ref
1. colour — yellow	36
2. weight — light	38
3. guess pine	40
4. check two-coloured	42
5. check no pores	43
6. check soft	45

output

Figure 5.8 *The transcript of a talk-through can be analysed to determine
knowledge and the way in which it is used.   Here a wood-carver is
examining a wooden plate*

67

a second expert to provide hypothetical cases, or suggested diagnoses for comment, to provoke discussion.

If the development team has decided to use a shell for the expert system, then the approach is necessarily different. This is analogous to the systems analyst's choice of package rather than a purpose-built program (Goodall 1985). In a shell the fundamental structure and inference mechanisms have been decided, and all that is required is the specific knowledge for the new system. Shells have proved very successful in many applications, and the existing structure means that the entering of the knowledge is relatively easy. However, shells can be restrictive if the knowledge domain does not closely match the particular design of the shell being used. For this reason it is desirable for the expert system shell to be chosen after several interviews have taken place, and not at the start of the project. The questioning methods can still be used to discover the knowledge which is to be entered into the shell. Some researchers have reported that a shell is useful for education and training purposes early in system development, but is usually discarded for the 'real' project.

Debugging

Debugging is the refinement of an existing formulation. This formulation can be a model on paper, or a simple computer-based system. Many of the tasks involved in this process have already been outlined.

Very early on the expert and knowledge engineer can exchange roles, so that the knowledge engineer does the diagnosis or decision-making. The expert can then criticize the process, and provide the missing information or correct any errors in the existing formulation. Alternatively, a second expert could comment on the findings to date. The knowledge engineer can also check models by simple observation of the expert at work.

When faults are located then they must be traced back to their origins. This must be done with care, recording both the changes and the reasons for them. The problems are similar to those of maintaining a database system. Information might be held in several places, and a choice must be made as to which of these need to be altered. Similarly, the consequences of insertion or deletion of information or rules should be investigated thoroughly before such changes are made. In the same way that computer programs should be modified by going back to the original design rather than by making *ad hoc* changes to coding, a knowledge base or inference mechanism should be changed cautiously, and at the design level. The importance of formally recording changes cannot be over-emphasized.

Summary

Interviews will play an important part in the knowledge acquisition process. Communication and inter-personal skills will be very important as the knowledge engineer and domain expert work together. All findings must be carefully recorded, checked and analysed. The knowledge engineer may have to prompt the expert, and should encourage him to describe his expertise in a way which is most natural to him. There are several questioning techniques known from psychology. The knowledge engineer should try to plan a structured approach to the questioning and to the analysis. Early feedback is important, and the expert should be encouraged to comment on intermediate findings and results. All findings should be kept and details of changes, errors and corrections must be kept for reference. The knowledge engineer must be versatile in his approach and maintain the interest of the expert and himself.

CHAPTER 6

Reasoning and probability theory

Decision-making usually involves the use of rules. Simple rules are acceptable to most people in their everyday life, e.g.

In the UK, if you are under 60 years of age then you are not entitled to a retirement pension.

A rule for entitlement might be more complex, but understandable, e.g.

If you are at least 60 years old and female and you have been resident in the UK for at least 25 years, or if you are male and at least 65 years old and you have been resident in the UK for at least 30 years then, provided you are not receiving a disability pension, you are entitled to the retirement pension.

Legislation consists of many hundreds of rules which need well-defined clauses and terms. People use 'if . . . then . . .' statements in conversation, and often use rules in their everyday life. However, problems which require expertise are not deterministic, i.e. the solutions cannot be stated in simple rules. Where judgement is involved, people often use words like probably, unlikely, almost certainly, i.e. uncertainty is involved. In some cases they quantify what they mean. For example:

There is a small risk, about 5%, that you have this disease; we'll do more tests to clarify the situation.

Your chances of passing this course are very slim — about 20%.

I am 99% confident that if you give the plant water its condition will improve.

The ways in which people use these percentages are ill defined, and often inconsistent. However, there is a rigorous mathematical theory of probability which provides a logical model for uncertainty. The next chapter mentions an alternative model for certainty measures.

The foundations of probability

Probability theory originated in the seventeenth century in the context of gambling. A gambler assesses his chance of winning and therefore the risk associated with his bid (Ehrenberg 1982). This process is very similar to that of an expert weighing up evidence, and judging whether he has sufficient evidence to justify a particular course of action. Chance, expectation and risk are components of both probability theory and expert judgements.

Probability is a measure of certainty between 0 and 1. The extreme values denote impossibility and certainty. (Pure mathematicians might argue about this definition, but it will suffice in this context.) Most people would understand that if a fair coin is tossed then the probability of its landing on a certain side is 0.5. This is because we ignore the possibility of its landing on its edge or not landing at all, and the other two outcomes are equally likely. Furthermore, only one of the events (head or tail) can occur at once, i.e. the events are *mutually exclusive*. This leads us to the classical definition of probability:

If a random experiment has N possible outcomes which are all equally likely and mutually exclusive, and n of these possibilities has outcome A then the probability of outcome A is n/N.

For example, consider a standard pack of 52 playing cards which has been shuffled so that the order of the cards is unpredictable. If a card is picked at random then the chance that it is a club is $13/52 = 0.25$. There are 52 cards, each of which is equally likely to be chosen.

There are 13 cards which are clubs.
Prob(card is club) = $13/52 = 0.25$.

This is a very simplistic view of uncertainty. The definition depends on the terms random, mutually exclusive and equally likely. It cannot help much with questions like:

What is the probability that a child born in London will be male?

What is the chance that the reported error in the computer hardware was transient?

What is the probability that the pain is caused by indigestion, and not a serious illness?

These are all real questions, and experts continually make similar judgements.

If we looked at the record of births in London over the past two years then we could calculate the relative frequency of male births, i.e. the ratio of number of boys to number of births. We would expect this to be close to the true probability. Assuming that there had been no genetic changes, a more reliable estimate could be obtained from the records of the past ten years. So, if we can imagine a series of observations under constant conditions then the probability p of event A can be approximated by the relative frequency of A in a series of such observations. In practice 'true' probabilities are almost impossible to quantify, and most probabilities used are estimates based on *relative frequencies.*

Venn diagrams are a convenient way of representing simple probability concepts. The totality of all possible outcomes, with a total probability of 1, is represented by a rectangle. Events are represented by circles within the rectangle. Events which are mutually exclusive are represented by circles which do not overlap, while other circles intersect. These features are illustrated in Figure 6.1. Note that in a pack of cards the events club and heart are mutually exclusive, whereas club and king are not. The event club is contained within black card, since all clubs are black.

universe

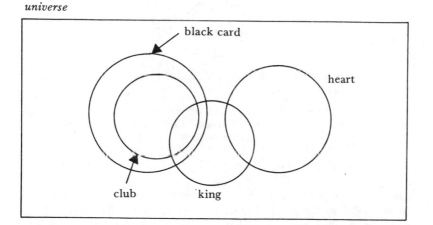

Figure 6.1 *Venn diagrams can be used to illustrate relationships between events. Here all clubs are black, some black cards are kings, and clubs and hearts are mutually exclusive.*

Combination of events

In most problems we are interested in probabilities involving more than one simple event or outcome. The event not A, denoted by A' is the complement of A and its probability is given by:

Prob(A') = 1 − Prob(A)

For example, when tossing a coin if A = head then A' = tail and:

Prob(tail) = 1 − Prob(head)

A and A' are clearly mutually exclusive and together describe the whole universe of outcomes. If a patient's symptoms indicate that he is suffering from cancer with chance 3% then the chance that he does not have cancer is 97%.

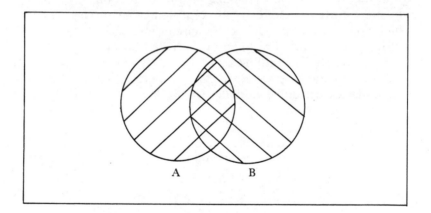

Figure 6.2 *A representation of the compound event A OR B; OR is inclusive, i.e. A OR B means A or B or both A and B. Prob(A OR B) = Prob(A) + Prob(B) − Prob(A AND B).*

Key: B only, A only, both A and B.

The compound event A OR B is represented in Figure 6.2. In probability theory OR is inclusive, i.e. A OR B means either A or B or both A and B.

Prob(A OR B) = Prob(A) + Prob(B) − Prob(A AND B)

Note that this reduces to:

Prob(A OR B) = Prob(A) + Prob(B)

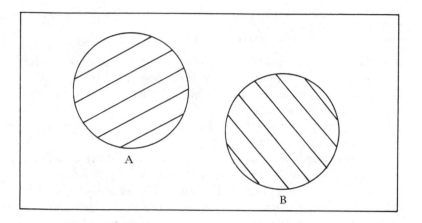

Figure 6.3 *Mutual exclusion: when A and B are mutually exclusive then Prob(A OR B) = Prob(A) + Prob(B).*

Key: A, B.

if, and only if, A and B are mutually exclusive, as in Figure 6.3. A and B are mutually exclusive means that Prob(A AND B) = 0. For example, in a pack of cards:

Prob(king OR heart)   = Prob(king) + Prob(heart) −
                        Prob(king AND heart)

                      = 4/52 + 13/52 − 1/52

                      = 16/52 = 0.31

The other compound event is AND. A AND B means both A and B together. Here the concept of independence is fundamentally important. In simple terms, two events are independent if our knowledge of the outcome of one does not influence our opinion of the other. In mathematical terms this is given by:

A and B are independent if and only if Prob(A AND B) = Prob(A) x Prob(B).

In a pack of cards the events king and heart are independent, because:

Prob(king) = 4/52
Prob(heart) = 13/52
Prob(king AND heart) = 1/52 = 4/52 x 13/52
                     = Prob(king) x Prob(heart).

However, the events red and club are not independent:

Prob(red) = 26/52
Prob(club) = 13/52
Prob(red AND club) = 0 (there is no red club)

If a patient suffers acute pain after eating then it is likely that he will lose weight, because he will eat less. In this case the events suffered pain and lost weight are not independent. This does not mean that pain is always accompanied by weight loss; either can occur without the other, but one tends to occur with the other.

On the other hand, consider a doctor prescribing a well-tested drug which has a known and very small risk of side effects. If one of his patients has just suffered these side effects, then on this evidence he has no reason to suspect that a different patient will also react to the drug. The two outcomes are independent.

Conditional probability is also a widely used measure. The conditional probability of A given B is defined by:

$$\text{Prob}(A|B) = \frac{\text{Prob}(A \text{ and } B)}{\text{Prob}(B)}, \text{ as long as Prob}(B) > 0$$

This measures the chance of A occurring given that we know B has occurred. In effect we are restricting our world of possibilities to the event B and considering that part of it which is both A and B. This is illustrated in Figure 6.4. Note that if A and B are independent then this reduces to:

$$\text{Prob}(A|B) = \text{Prob}(A)$$

i.e. knowledge about B does not influence our opinion of A. Independence is one of the most important concepts in probability theory.

Probability distributions

So far we have considered the general principles of probability where the outcomes are categorical, or discrete. Probability can be applied in many different types of problem. We use the term 'random variable' to describe an event which can be described by a real number. A *discrete random variable* can take values which are discrete and can be listed, e.g. the number of people who will die in the next month is a discrete variable; it can take values 0, 1, 2, 3 . . .

A variable which is not discrete is continuous, and is often a measurement, e.g. height, specific gravity. For a *continuous variable* it is usually meaningless to talk about the probability that it takes a specific value, e.g. Prob(X=3.2). There are infinitely many possible values, so the chance of any one of them must be zero. In this case a range of values is used, e.g. Prob(2.8 < X < 3.2).

There are a number of commonly used models or patterns depicting the way in which random variables behave. For discrete distributions this involves giving the probability for each possible outcome value, e.g. Poisson distribution:

$$\text{Prob}(X = n) = \frac{e^{-m}m^n}{n!}$$

where n = 0, 1, 2 . . .
and m is a fixed parameter of the distribution.

For continuous variables it is usual to define a probability density function f(x) which describes a curve. The probability that the variable takes values in a certain range is the area under the curve (this is illustrated in Figure 6.5) in that range, e.g. normal distribution:

$$f(x) = \frac{e^{\left(\frac{-1/2(x-\mu)^2}{\sigma^2}\right)}}{\sqrt{2\pi\sigma}}$$

where x is a real value and μ and σ are parameters.

(It is not the purpose of this text to give details of specific distributions, and the interested reader is advised to consult a text on probability and statistics.)

There are various parameters used to describe distributions. In general, there are two features of interest: average and variability. The *average*, or *mean*, of a distribution describes the expected value of the random variable, i.e. in some way a typical value. Another important feature is the *spread* or *variability* about the mean. If there is a lot of uncertainty in the data then the variability is high and it is likely that the random variable will take values away from the mean.

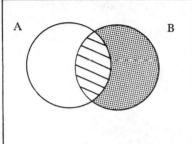

$$\text{Prob}(A \mid B) = \frac{\text{Prob}(A \text{ AND } B)}{\text{Prob}(B)}$$

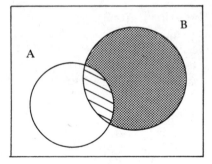

A given B is unlikely

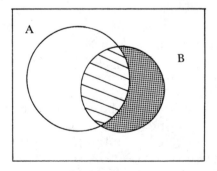

A given B is likely

Figure 6.4 *Conditional probability: Prob(A | B) measures the likelihood of event A given that we know event B is true.*

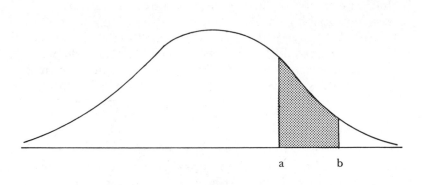

a   b

Figure 6.5 *The behaviour of a real variable is modelled by a probability density function. The probability of a value lying between a and b is the area under that part of the curve. The area under the whole curve is 1.0.*

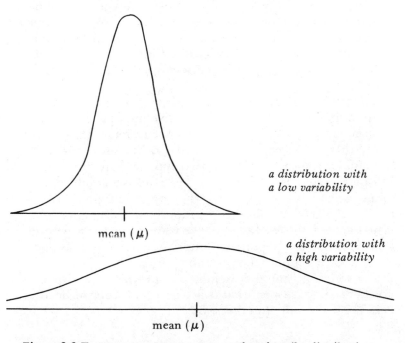

a distribution with a low variability

mean (μ)

a distribution with a high variability

mean (μ)

Figure 6.6 *Two common parameters used to describe distributions are the mean and variance. Variance measures the spread or variability about the mean.*

If the variability is low then the values of the random variable will be clustered close to the mean. Figure 6.6 illustrates mean and variability. A *normal distribution* with a small variance has a curve which is a tall thin bell-shape; a normal distribution with a high variance has a wide flat bell-shape. The mean determines the location of the curve. For a normal distribution μ is a mean and σ a measure of spread. A normal distribution is commonly used to model real variables.

Statistical tests

One common use of statistics is to test hypotheses. When performing a test we have two hypotheses; we carry out an experiment and decide in favour of one or other of them. A jury behaves like this. A defendant is assumed innocent until proven guilty. The two hypotheses are 'defendant is innocent', and 'defendant is guilty'. The jury's experiment is an investigation of evidence produced by the defence and witnesses. If the evidence against the defendant is strong then he will probably be found guilty; otherwise he will be found to be innocent. There are two types of mistake which can be made: to find an innocent man guilty and to find a guilty man innocent. If the jury is inclined to be harsh then innocent men will tend to be convicted; if it is lenient then guilty men will go free.

The process of statistical testing is very similar. We have a null hypothesis H_0 and an alternative hypothesis H_1. If our experiment gives us sufficient evidence to reject H_0 in favour of H_1 then we accept the alternative; otherwise we accept the null hypothesis. There are two types of error: type I error is to reject H_0 when H_0 is true (this is a conditional event) given by $\text{Prob}(\text{reject } H_0 | H_0 \text{ true})$; the type II error is $\text{Prob}(\text{accept } H_0 | H_0 \text{ false})$. It is usual to fix the chance of a type I error to be 5% (or 1% if we want to be strict) and therefore the null hypothesis tends to be favoured (as does the innocent verdict on a prisoner).

For example, suppose we have a coin which we suspect is not fair, i.e. we suspect that it is biased in favour of heads, say. Then our null hypothesis is:

$$H_0 : \text{coin is fair, i.e. Prob(head)} = 1/2$$
$$H_1 : \text{coin is not fair, i.e. Prob(head)} > 1/2$$

We carry out an experiment of tossing the coin ten times, and report nine occurrences of a head. For a fair coin we would have expected about five heads. What is the probability (given the null hypothesis) of getting a result at least this bad? We need to evaluate the chance of a result this far away from the expected results, under H_0, i.e. nine or ten heads, given that Prob(head) = 0.5.

Prob(nine heads OR ten heads | coin fair)
= Prob(nine heads | coin fair) + Prob(ten heads | coin fair)
= 0.00098   + 0.0098
= 0.01

This is less than 5% — the level of the test. The chance of getting such a result with an unbiased coin is about 1%. The result is said to be *highly significant*, and we conclude that there is evidence that the coin is biased in favour of heads.

We can extend these methods to other problems. For example, suppose we suspected that high blood pressure was a symptom of a particular disease. Our hypotheses might be:

$H_0 : M_D = M_{D'}$ and $H_1 : M_D > M_{D'}$

where M_D is the average blood pressure of people with the disease, and $M_{D'}$ the average of those without.

Our experiments would be to measure the blood pressure of two groups of suitably chosen patients: one group suffering from the disease and the other not. A suitable test would be to calculate the observed average value for each group and then the difference. The fact that the observed average for diseased people was higher would not be sufficient evidence in itself. The difference would be significant only if it were too big to have occurred by chance under the null hypothesis. This test would require assumptions about the distribution of the variable blood pressure.

This subject is a complex one. For the present purposes we have demonstrated how probability forms a rigorous basis for deciding between alternatives when measurements arc subject to variation. We compare expected results with observed results, and reject our original hypothesis if the difference is too large to have happened reasonably by chance. The intrinsic uncertainty means that we cannot be

81

absolutely sure of our results. It must be added that statisticians are divided in their approach to tests. We have presented the classical view: there is a rival theory based on Bayesian statistics.

Correlation

The term 'correlated' has a special meaning in statistics. Given two random variables X and Y it is possible to calculate their *correlation coefficient*, which is a measure of the linear relationship between X and Y. The formula is not given here, but examples of patterns of observations and the corresponding correlation coefficients are given in Figure 6.7.

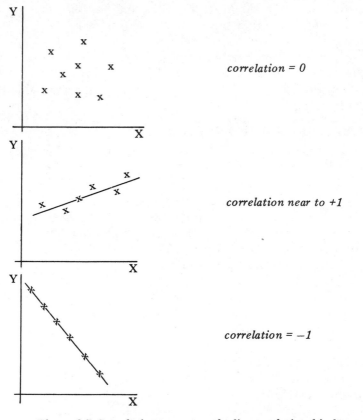

Figure 6.7 *Correlation measures the linear relationship between two variables. It does not imply independence or cause and effect, but can be useful to suggest patterns in data.*

A correlation coefficient of 0 indicates no linear relationship. If X and Y are independent then their correlation coefficient is zero. However, a coefficient of zero does not imply independence.

A correlation coefficient near +1 indicates that when X takes larger values Y tends to take larger values, and X is small when Y is small. In this case there is evidence for a linear relationship between the variables.

A correlation coefficient near −1 indicates that when X takes larger values Y tends to take smaller values, and X is smaller when Y is larger. Here there is evidence for a linear relationship with a negative gradient.

Height and weight tend to be positively correlated, because taller people are likely to be heavier. However, it is possible to be tall and light, or short and heavy. Weight and fitness will be negatively correlated: an overweight person will not be very fit.

Correlation does not imply cause and effect, and is often misinterpreted in this context. However, when exploring data and selecting attributes to describe different types of problems (for induction, for example) correlation can be very useful. The importance of correlated variables is also mentioned on page 122. Symptoms or attributes of a state tend to occur together. It is often necessary to discuss correlation in qualitative terms, even if it is impossible to calculate the correlation coefficient.

Bayes theorem
Bayes theorem has been used extensively in expert systems development. In its simplest form it is:

$$\text{Prob}(H|E) = \text{Prob}(E|H)\,\frac{\text{Prob}(H)}{\text{Prob}(E)}$$

where H is an hypothesis and E some evidence, e.g. H could be the hypothesis that a particular disease is present, and E could be the symptoms which have been observed. The formula relates the prior probability Prob(H) with the posterior probability Prob(H | E), i.e. the new probability in the light of evidence. Prob(H) is the initial estimate without any information about E. Prob(H | E) is our new probability when we know that E is true. Our judgement is affected by knowledge about the symptoms, i.e. event E.

In practice it is not the probabilities which are used, but odds. The odds in favour of hypothesis H are given by the ratio:

$$\frac{\text{Prob}(H)}{\text{Prob}(H')}$$

So, using Bayes' formula the odds are related by:

$$(\text{odds given E}) = \frac{\text{Prob}(E|H)}{\text{Prob}(E|H')} \times (\text{initial odds})$$

The terms on the right hand side of this equation must be estimated in some way. However, this is not trivial. The evidence E is unlikely to be simply one observation or event. E will usually be the compound event given by:

$$E = E_1 \text{ AND } E_2 \text{ AND} \ldots \text{AND } E_K$$

so the probabilities required depend on the joint distribution of symptoms; this will be complex, and seldom known. To overcome this problem many implementations have assumed that the Es are sufficiently independent that:

$$\text{Prob}(E_1 \text{ AND } E_2 \ldots \text{AND } E_K|H)$$

can be written as:

$$\text{Prob}(E_1|H) \cdot \text{Prob}(E_2|H) \ldots \text{Prob}(E_K|H)$$

There is little evidence to support this simplification; however, it simplifies the odds equation to:

$$(\text{odds given evidence}) = \frac{\text{Prob}(E_1|H)}{\text{Prob}(E_1|H')} \cdot \frac{\text{Prob}(E_2|H)}{\text{Prob}(E_2|H')}$$

$$\ldots \frac{\text{Prob}(E_K|H)}{\text{Prob}(E_K|H')} \times (\text{initial odds})$$

i.e. it is simply the product of the individual odds ratios.

The simplification can cause gross errors in computation, and the error tends to increase with number of evidences. In fact, the errors can be so great that the entire model becomes unusable. It is the relationships between joint symptoms and the disease which are important. For example, each individual symptom may have a very low correlation with the disease, but the joint occurrence of many symptoms might be highly indicative of the disease. The over-simplification of the Bayesian model contorts the data, and a discussion about patterns and relationships is, in general, more fruitful.

Problems of estimation

Probability and statistical theory can be used in at least two ways in knowledge acquisition. If data are available in the form of case histories or documented statistics, then statistical tests can be carried out to identify patterns or possible rules from the data, or to support and test statements made by the expert. This can be used to determine relationships between observed variables or between symptoms and states. Relative frequencies or averages can be used to estimate probabilities and typical values, and estimates of variance give indications of the accuracy of such estimates.

If the knowledge engineer decides that the knowledge is to be represented with probabilities in the inference mechanism (e.g. using Bayes' rule) then probability estimates must be obtained. However, in most cases it is necessary for the expert to offer values which cannot always be verified.

The problems of using probability models are compounded by the fact that people do not really understand the theory (Johnson-Laird & Wason 1977). An expert's estimate of probability can be wildly inaccurate, and difficult to elicit or justify. If Bayes' theorem is being used in an expert system one of the main problems is continually adjusting the odds estimates until the results are reasonable. The three common estimates for probability are 0, 0.5 and 1, or numbers very close to them. People find it difficult to estimate probabilities with any confidence except for the three cases of impossibility, certainty and complete uncertainty (i.e. the values 0, 1 and 0.5) (Scholz 1983).

There are methods of eliciting probabilities (Welbank 1983), but none has proved universally acceptable. One method is to provide a simple illustration of a random event so that the expert can compare two values. If the knowledge engineer has a disc coloured black and white where the ratio of black to white can be changed, and the disc can be spun

85

so that a pointer lands in the black area with probability p, then p can be adjusted to any value between 0 and 1. The value of p can be changed according to the expert's answer to the question: 'Is the chance of this event greater than, less than, or equal to the chance of the pointer landing on black for this disc?' The probability elicited is the value of p when the expert is happy that the two probabilities are equal.

These methods do not overcome misunderstandings about probabilities associated with compound events. The main problem with forcing the expert to describe his inference in terms of probability theory is that the theory is not his natural method of reasoning. This means that the estimates will be inaccurate, and the process may confuse the expert's view of his knowledge and distort it.

Two examples are included here to illustrate common misunderstandings:

1) 5% of the population has cancer.
   If you have cancer you are 99% certain to have pain.
   40% of the population complains of this pain.
   A patient has the pain, what is the chance that he has cancer?

2) Out of ten mature students nine passed the exam.
   Out of 50 ordinary students 35 passed the exam.
   Given a student who passed, what is the probability that he was mature?

The answers are 1) 12% and 2) 20%. Many people's guesses are wildly wrong.

Summary

This chapter has described the basis of probability theory. The theory itself is consistent and correct, but in order to apply it we need to make assumptions about underlying distributions and independence. Statistical tests are a method of using probability theory to judge the weight of evidence and of selecting an hypothesis from two alternatives. However, many of the theorems and methods needed when using probabilities in expert systems require the expert to estimate probabilities, sometimes without recourse to relative frequencies. There is evidence that many people do not have an intuitive understanding of the laws of probability, and so estimates are likely to be very inaccurate. Furthermore, simplification of formulae can cause gross errors in computation.

These problems should not preclude the knowledge engineer from using statistical methods in data exploration; unfortunately, many have completely ignored the wealth of theory from the subject. This seems extremely foolish. It is advantageous for the knowledge engineer to have an understanding of the principles of probability and statistics, although it is dangerous to force an expert to represent uncertainty wholly in terms of probabilities, unless the expert finds such a method easy and natural.

CHAPTER 7

Fuzziness in reasoning

People reason with words, not numbers. This may be why we find probability theory counter-intuitive, and in some cases difficult to understand. The many shades of meaning which give language its richness and colour contrast with the precise rigour of mathematical theory, logic and computer languages. Whilst knowledge elicitation is essentially distinct from the subsequent knowledge representation, the eliciter is almost certain to be influenced by his anticipation of how he is to represent judgement and uncertainty. This chapter examines some aspects of vagueness, together with alternative models of uncertainty.

Usage of words
There is a difference between the meaning and the usage of words. Owing to a change in usage the meaning of some words has changed over a period of years. It is not the strict dictionary definition of a word which is important, but the way in which the expert uses a word. He may not even be able to define a particular word, though usually he will be able to give an example of a use. Technical terms are relatively easy to define. Commonly used words are less easy to define, either in abstract or even in context. For example, consider the word 'cold'. What is the criterion for saying that the weather is cold? The answer depends on the temperature, and almost certainly also on the time of year. A cold summer's day can be milder than a warm winter's day. Similarly, a big mouse will be smaller than a tiny elephant. It is relatively easy to quote examples of cold days and days which are not cold, but more difficult to give a definitive rule. There is a vagueness or *fuzziness* about a certain range of temperatures; they might constitute coldness,

and they might not. A rule such as 'temperature < X' is too simplistic. This is one of the reasons why the output from an inductive program must be investigated carefully; such rules tend to be crisp and simple (this is also discussed on pages 114-126).

Fuzziness

Everyone uses fuzzy words, and seldom question whether they or others understand their usage of those words. An individual may not be consistent in his own use of words, and there is even less chance that someone else has the same usage. As examples consider the words 'most', 'probably' and 'believed'. When a group of people was asked about the definition of the term 'most', there were two types of response:

'Anything over 50% — that is a majority.'

and,

'About 75%, perhaps more. Typical in some way. It's difficult to give a number — it's high.'

When asked to rank 'believed' and 'probably' in terms of strength of belief, the two opposing views were:

' "Probably" is stronger. "Believed" means that I would believe it without much evidence, like an act of faith. "Probably" means you have some evidence, so it's more likely.'

and,

'I wouldn't believe it if it wasn't probable, so "believed" is stronger. Probability is vague anyway.'

Nevertheless, we all use words expressing belief when we are reasoning or arguing. Consider the following example which is a quote from a doctor:

'I wouldn't expect that disease in a young girl of 20. It's so rare as to be negligible. It isn't worth carrying out the tests on a young person. If they're young I'd most likely not do the tests. If they're older I probably would do them.'

The doctor is using vague rules. Some fuzzy words which he uses are young, older, negligible, (so) rare, most likely, probably. When pressed to define such words, experts often find it extremely difficult.

90

IF . . . THEN rules

There are models of plausible reasoning (Polya 1969) based on the clear rule:

IF A THEN B

These models define patterns which can be used sensibly in argument. If the knowledge engineer is aware of such models then it is easier to elicit the knowledge in a form which the expert recognizes and understands. All too often, it is tempting to ask for probabilities or strengths of belief, ignoring the expert's own pattern of inference. During elicitation the anticipation of representation should not dictate the form of discussion between knowledge engineer and expert, but the eliciter must be able to recognize logical and illogical reasoning (Ellis 1979).

The crisp mathematical rules are easily defined. The basis for a rule (Quine 1972) is:

$$\text{IF A THEN B} \quad \text{or} \quad A \Rightarrow B$$

This states that if A is true then B is necessarily true also. It does not state that B implies A, and B can be true with A false. It is difficult to find a clear example of this concept except in the context of mathematics, for example:

$$\text{if } X = 2 \text{ then } X^2 = 4$$

Note that $X^2 = 4$ does not mean that X is the value 2; $X = -2$ is another solution. The rule is exactly equivalent to:

$$\text{NOT B} \Rightarrow \text{NOT A}$$

Unfortunately, in common usage 'if' and 'only if' are interchanged and used improperly. Strictly, the definitions are given by:

B if A means $\quad A \Rightarrow B$
B only if A means $B \Rightarrow A$
B if and only if A means $A \Rightarrow B$ and $B \Rightarrow A$, written $A \Leftrightarrow B$

These three cases are illustrated in Figure 7.1. Note that for the IF rule B can be true when A is false, and for the ONLY IF rule A can be true with B false. This is illustrated by the circles lying within each other; only for IF AND ONLY IF are A and B the same, i.e. the circles are on top of each other.

Statements based on logic are made more complex by the use of AND and OR. AND is easy to understand, but OR is ambiguous. If a child is told 'You can have sweets or an

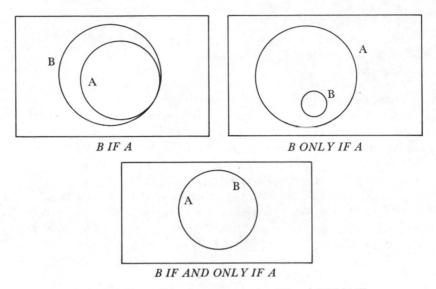

Figure 7.1 *Venn diagrams representing IF and ONLY IF.*

ice cream', he will usually understand that he is not allowed both. This is an exclusive OR. The statement 'The leaves on the tree are green or yellow' implies that possibly some leaves are green and others are yellow. This is an inclusive OR: yellow and green can occur together. The English language does not distinguish between these two meanings, and the interpretation may depend on the context. In formal logic and computer logic, the inclusive OR is more common. The knowledge engineer must be aware of the possible ambiguity, and clarify statements where necessary. Further ambiguities arise when both terms AND and OR are used in the same statement (Gane & Sarson 1979). For example, consider the rule:

'If the patient is over 40 and has high blood pressure or is female then I would refer them'.

Does this statement mean:

'If the patient is over 40 and has high blood pressure or if the patient is over 40 and is female then I would refer them'.

or does it mean:

'If the patient is over 40 and has high blood pressure or if the patient is female then I would refer them'.

Only the person who made the statement can identify the
correct interpretation. Note that the two interpretations
give potentially different outcomes for a female patient
under the age of 40. Again, in computer logic the meaning is
unambiguous — the problem arises because of the way we use
words. In systems analysis some people use *structured
English* to try to overcome this problem.

EXAMPLES
Let us examine some rules, and their meaning.

RULE: 'If the test is positive then you have glandular fever.'

This rule means that:

1) A positive result indicates glandular fever.
2) If you do not have glandular fever then the test will not
   be positive.
3) It is possible to have glandular fever without the test
   being positive, so a negative result does not mean that
   you do not have glandular fever.

RULE: 'If the student does not have the minimum requirements then
he cannot have an offer of a place.'

This rule implies:

1) If a student has an offer then he has the minimum entry
   requirements.
2) It might be possible to have the minimum entry
   requirements but not get a definite offer.

We can summarize this by:

$A \Rightarrow B$
A is true means B is true
B is false means A is false

Knowing that B is true tells us nothing definite about A.
However, knowing that B is true might strengthen our belief
that A might be true, because B is a symptom, cause, or
indicator of A.

Symptoms
Much judgement and reasoning using vague rules involve
weighing up the strength of evidence in symptoms (see Polya
1969). For example:

'Ménière's disease causes spells of dizziness.'

is a rule of the form:

If A then B

i.e. if you have Ménière's disease then you will have spells of dizziness.

If we are told that a patient has spells of dizziness then it is more credible that he has Ménière's disease. However, dizziness can be caused by other illnesses or disorders. If dizziness is a common ailment for this type of patient then we do not have much evidence for Ménière's disease, but if it is rare except as a consequence of the disease, then our inference is stronger. The strength of our inference depends on how likely B is in itself. If B is very common, then we have little evidence for A; if B is very rare then A becomes much more credible. So B is true makes A more credible is our vague rule. Further examples are:

RULE: 'If the battery is flat then the car won't start.'

This gives us the vague rule: if the car won't start then it is more credible that the battery is flat.

Based on 'If you are pregnant then you will put on weight', we can say: 'You have put on weight so it is (slightly) more credible that you are pregnant'. Note that in this case the inference here is very weak without further evidence. Sometimes, as in this example, the symptom can be countermanded by other facts, e.g. if the patient were male or over the age of 60 then a gain in weight would not lead us to consider pregnancy. This rather trivial example shows how the misuse of rules can lead to illogical and unfounded inference, particularly when it is based on a small number of evidences. This is illustrated in Figure 7.2; one diagram shows the case of strong inference, and the other is very weak.

In practice, there is usually more than one symptom, or evidence, i.e. the rule is:

$$A \Rightarrow B_1, B_2, \ldots B_n$$

For example:

'Ménière's disease causes spells of dizziness, tinnitus, and progressive hearing loss.'

Evidence of a single symptom B_i tells us little about A. However, a plausible line of reasoning is:

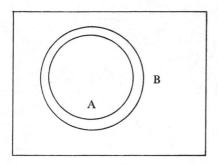

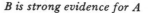
B is strong evidence for A

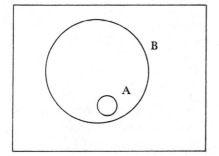

B is weak evidence for A

Figure 7.2 *B TRUE makes A more credible.*
In each of these two cases the rule is IF A THEN B;
in one case B is strong evidence for A, in the other it is not.

'B_3 is true. I also know that B_1 and B_2 are true, and that B_3 is different from them. So this makes A more credible.'

So a doctor may argue:

'Dizziness on its own is not very strong evidence for Ménière's disease. But you are a young person and so it is unlikely to be caused by natural deterioration. The fact that you also complain of tinnitus — the buzzing in the ears — is more evidence. Also you do seem to have some loss of hearing. That all together speaks of Ménière's disease, and I'll try you on these tablets.'

This pattern of inference is illustrated in Figure 7.3. This form of reasoning is the one which is often represented by Bayes' rule (as described in Chapter 6). The weights of evidence used in the doctor's diagnosis are not independent; it is the combination of symptoms which gives credibility to his solution. In Figure 7.3 circle A is within each of the three

95

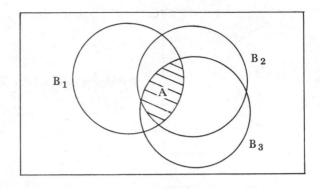

Figure 7.3 *The rule IF A THEN B_i holds for i = 1, 2, 3.*
Each B_i is weak evidence for A, but B_1 AND B_2 AND B_3.
is strong evidence for A.
Key: \\\\\\ B_1 and B_2 and B_3

areas B_1, B_2 and B_3. Being within B_i is, in itself, little
evidence for A. Being in all of the Bs is strong evidence for A.

The knowledge engineer must take special note of the
ways in which combinations of symptoms are used; this
frequently forms the basis of the knowledge handling.
It is also here that the problems of representing the inference
manifest themselves.

Weak rules

Some rules are not as simple as A => B. A common rule is
A can cause B, or A usually causes B. In this case A does not
necessarily imply B. Given the rule:

A CAN CAUSE B

our patterns of inference are therefore weaker, and given by:

A TRUE makes B more credible
B FALSE makes A less credible
A credible makes B slightly more credible
B true makes A slightly more credible, etc.

For example, if the weak rule is:

'An irritable bowel will often cause violent abdominal pain.'

Then our inference models are:

1) If you have an irritable bowel then it is credible that you will
experience violent abdominal pain.

96

2) If you do not have abdominal pain then it is less credible that you have an irritable bowel.
3) If you have abdominal pain then it is slightly more credible that you have an irritable bowel.

This is illustrated in Figure 7.4. In this case circle A is not contained wholly within circle B; inference is similar to that shown in Figure 7.2, but is weaker.

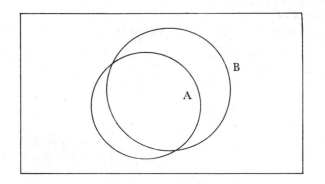

Figure 7.4 *This illustrates the weaker form of a rule;*
A CAN CAUSE B. Here the circles overlap but A is not within B.
The inference patterns are therefore weaker.

Incompatibility

Another form of reasoning, based on a slight change to the basic rule, involves incompatibilities:

A is incompatible with B

This means that A and B cannot be true together, given by the rule:

If A THEN NOT B   or   A ⇒ NOT B

Possible combinations are:

A true   B false
A false   B true
A false   B false

Our patterns of inference are:

A is true means B is false
A is credible means B is less credible
B is false means A is more credible

97

For example:

'A patient cannot be both sterile and pregnant.'

1) A sterile patient cannot be pregnant.
2) A pregnant patient cannot be sterile.
3) If a patient is not pregnant then it is more credible that she is sterile.

Again, the weight of inference depends on the degree of association between the two events A and NOT B. This is illustrated in Figure 7.5. In one case NOT B is almost the same area as A so the inference is strong; in the other NOT B is a large area apart from A so the inference is weak.

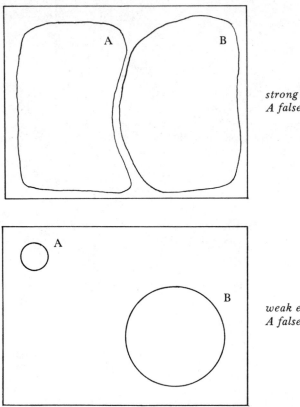

strong evidence:
A false means B true

weak evidence:
A false means B true

Figure 7.5 *Incompatibility: IF A THEN NOT B.*
If A is false then B is more credible; one diagram shows strong inference and the other weak inference.

98

Analogies

In making judgements we often make analogies, e.g. 'This applicant reminds me very much of a student a few years ago. He did very well on the course, so most probably this one would too.' This model of pattern-matching, where the expert compares a new problem with a very similar one to which he knows the answer, is appealing. The form of reasoning is:

B is like A
A is true makes B more credible
A is false makes B less credible

This pattern is very fuzzy, and the expert should be able to clarify the situation by describing the characteristics of **B** which make it resemble **A**. However, pattern-matching is a very popular technique in AI work, and some experts seem to work by comparing new problems with a *bank* of typical case histories which they have remembered. If the new problem matches one in the bank then the solutions are similar. If a knowledge engineer detects this form of reasoning then he should try to discover the expert's bank of examples and his methods of pattern-matching.

Uncertainty in data

The vagueness or uncertainty which is an intrinsic feature of judgement is not unique to rules. Data presented to an expert or expert system can also be uncertain. Some data are clear facts with a yes/no answer, for example:

The applicant is over the age of 18

but others may be fuzzy:

The patient may have suffered from indigestion

So expertise involves dealing with uncertain data, and uncertain inference rules using those data. Much of the skill in judgement lies in weighing up the relative merits of data, facts, guesses and hypotheses, etc. (Lehrer 1974; Scholz 1983), and using a plausible line of reasoning with them. There are essentially two aspects to this uncertainty: belief and value. *Belief* is analogous to probability and measures the level of credibility. Probability is a numerical measure, as described in Chapter 6. People generally use words to express belief. There are over 50 terms in the English language expressing belief, and the number can be increased by qualifiers such as very, extremely, etc. However, if a subset of these terms could be agreed upon, together with an hierarchy expressing the relationships between them, then there is no reason why the expert should not be able to express his knowledge in simple English, which is 'natural' to him. For example, Figure 7.6 is a simple hierarchy showing the relationships between terms such as possible, certain and definite. A term low down on the hierarchy is stronger than one higher up. So 'certain' is stronger than 'probable', and 'proved' implies 'definite'. The main problem with this is ascertaining whether the expert is consistent in his usage of words, and whether the agreed relationships make sense to other people.

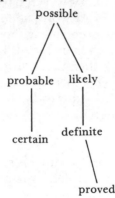

Figure 7.6 *It might be possible to draw an hierarchy representing the relationships between words expressing belief. This could be implemented in an expert system which was able to reason with words.*

The other element, that of *value*, is analogous to risk. Terms expressing value are those such as fatal, serious, dangerous, undesirable, etc. A possibility which is considered likely and serious may warrant immediate investigation, whereas one which is highly probable and undesirable may not. It will be necessary to draw up similar diagrams representing relationships between words describing risk or value as well, if the uncertainty handling is to be written in words. If the expert can do this then it will usually be a valuable exercise. The problem with using words is that there is such an abundance to choose from, but the advantage is that language is easy for the expert to use. Finally, in a logic language such as PROLOG it is easy to define beliefs and values with rules like:

IF patient could-have disease and disease is dangerous
THEN do tests

Implementation is less direct in more traditional computer languages, but this should not prevent the knowledge engineer from writing rules in a logical form of English. They can be converted into probabilities later, if required. The expert is far more likely to be able to talk in ordinary language than in terms of probabilities.

Endorsements

Several authorities have commented (Johnson-Laird & Wason 1977; Cohen 1985) on the disadvantages of a probabilistic approach to uncertainty. An alternative line of approach is to use *endorsements*, which keep reasons for, as well as degrees of, belief. Research in this area is being carried out in the form of an AI program called SOLOMON.

There will usually be evidence for and evidence against any hypothesis at a particular time. The decision as to which outweighs the other depends on both the kind of evidence and the quality of that evidence. This uses ideas similar to belief and risk. As illustrated in Figure 7.7, judgement may have to be made on the basis of, for example, a deduction and an assumption in favour, and prior knowledge and reported symptoms against. For the purposes of knowledge elicitation the most important feature of these results is a reminder to elicit and record reasons for belief, as well as degrees of belief. The expert will, at any time, select the path which he likes best; this will almost certainly be the best endorsed path. He will have opinions on matters such as the adequacy of propositions, the supportiveness of evidence, and the general usefulness of information. The knowledge engineer should record and use any such endorsements, and question the expert carefully about them.

Fuzzy logic

Whilst numerical models for belief have obvious disadvantages, it cannot be denied that the most famous expert systems

101

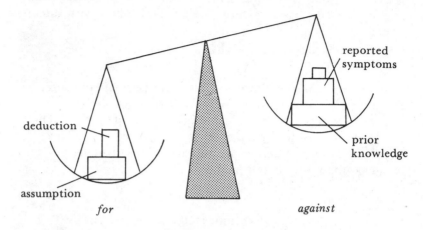

Figure 7.7 *Weighing up evidence for and against an hypothesis may involve consideration of the kind of evidence and its quality.*

do use them. Pure probability theory has been considered inadequate, and some famous systems use *certainty factors*. There has been a lot of debate about the meaning of these certainty factors, or degrees of belief, and also about the validity of their use. They appear as numbers between 0 and 1 (or in some cases between −1 and +1), associated with rules or data. Sometimes they can be interpreted as probabilities, and sometimes as degrees of importance or measures of confidence. They are very like membership values in fuzzy logic, and so it seems appropriate to give a brief outline of the theory of fuzzy logic, which is gaining in popularity.

Fuzzy sets
Fuzzy set theory and fuzzy logic were formulated by Zadeh, and have since been applied to many problems where traditional crisp logic and mathematics are inappropriate because of the inherent uncertainty (Mamdani & Gaines 1981; Van Ryzin 1977). In traditional logic a proposition is true or false; in fuzzy logic it has a degree of truth. For example, consider the question:

Is the object black? (or white?)

In crisp logic the answer can be either yes (black) or no (white). In fuzzy logic an object would be given a degree of blackness, where 0 indicates 'definitely not' and 1 indicates 'definitely'. An off-white object could be measured by 0.2, say, and a grey object by 0.6. This would not mean that one was three times as black as the other, but would enable the members of a set to be ranked. Let U be the universe of discourse or domain:

$$U = U_1 + U_2 + \ldots U_n$$

So U is the set of n objects $U_1, U_2 \ldots U_n$ which we are considering. A fuzzy set F is described by its members and their degrees of membership to that set, for example:

$$F = M_1/U_1 + M_2/U_2 \ldots + M_n/U_n$$

$U_1, U_2 \ldots U_n$ are members with degrees of membership $M_1, M_2 \ldots M_n$, and + denotes union, not addition. In other words this equation is a way of listing the various members together with their degrees of membership. Equivalently, F is given by:

$$F = \Sigma M_F(U_i)/U_i$$

where Σ denotes 'the set of'. We also define the fuzzy versions of union (inclusive OR), intersection (AND) and complement (NOT).

The grade of membership of U in the union FUG (F OR G) is at least that of its membership in the individual sets F, G. We do not know any more than this, and so the grade of membership is given by the maximum of the two. So:

$$F \cup G = \Sigma M_F(U)VM_G(U)/U$$

where V denotes maximum. The grade of membership of U in F∩G (F AND G) can be no greater than the membership in each of F and G. So intersection is defined by:

$$F n G = \Sigma M_F(U) \wedge M_G(U)/U$$

where $\wedge$ denotes minimum. The value 1 denotes full membership and 0 no membership. The complement of F, F' is given by:

$$F' = \Sigma (1 - M_F(U))/U$$

Notice how these formulae differ from the corresponding ones in probability for OR and AND.

103

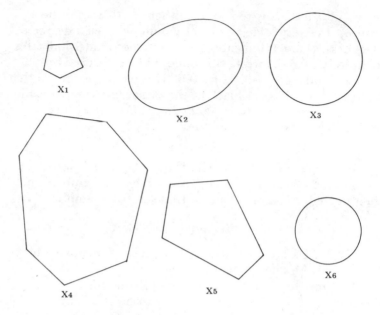

Figure 7.8 *This set of six figures can be described in terms of their size and shape by their fuzzy membership values in the sets Large and Round.*

Consider the objects in Figure 7.8 where the universe is the six objects X_1, X_2, X_3 ... X_6. If L is the fuzzy set of large shapes, and R the fuzzy set of round shapes then L and R could be defined by:

$L = 0.1/X_1 + 0.6/X_2 + 0.6/X_3 + 0.8/X_4 + 0.4/X_5 + 0.2/X_6$
$R = 0.1/X_1 + 0.7/X_2 + 1.0/X_3 + 0.5/X_4 + 0.1/X_5 + 1.0/X_6$

$L \cup R$ is the set of objects which are large or round. X_1 is not really large and not particularly round, so its membership in $L \cup R$ is low. X_6 is not large but perfectly round so its membership in large or round is 1.

$L \cup R = 0.1/X_1 + 0.7/X_2 + 1.0/X_3 + 0.8/X_4 + 0.4/X_5 + 1.0/X_6$

$L \cap R$ is the set of objects which are large and round

$L \cap R = 0.1/X_1 + 0.6/X_2 + 0.6/X_3 + 0.5/X_4 + 0.1/X_5 + 0.2/X_6$

In this case X_5 and X_6 have low membership values for large and round ($L \cap R$) because membership in at least one of L and R is low. The strongest membership is for X_2 and X_3 both of which have fairly high membership in both L and in R together.

104

L$'$ is the set of not large (i.e. small) objects

$$L' = 0.9/X_1 + 0.4/X_2 + 0.4/X_3 + 0.2/X_4 + 0.6/X_5 + 0.8/X_6$$

So X_1 has a high membership in L$'$ and X_4 has a low membership. The different membership values mean that it is not sensible to count the members in a fuzzy set. Instead we define the power P of a set F by:

$$P(F) = \Sigma\ M_F(X)$$

So, in Figure 7.8:

P(L)   =   2.7
P(R)   =   3.4
P(LUR) =   4.0

Applications of fuzzy logic
Given these basic definitions, together with extensions, it is possible to modify many results and methods of traditional set theory and logic. It is not the purpose of this text to give a comprehensive account of the uses of fuzzy set theory, but rather to indicate that the knowledge engineer is not constrained by the limitations of crisp logic. Suppose we have a rule:

IF (X AND Y) OR Z THEN T

and we cannot make exact statements about the truth of X, Y and Z. If we have subjective possibility values, x, y and z for X, Y and Z, then we should be able to assess the possibility of T. Using x as a membership value for X, and so on, we would have:

$t = (x \wedge y) \vee z$

Possible values and results are shown in Figure 7.9. The strength of belief in T depends on the weakest link in the logic. Notice how fuzzy logic makes no assumptions about any relationships between X, Y and Z.

Fuzzy set membership values can be used to represent linguistic values for a very simple grammar. Let the domain U of possible membership values be:

$U = 0 + 0.1 + 0.3 + 0.5 + 0.7 + 0.9 + 1$

and suppose we wish to define the terms high, medium and low. There is no single membership value which precisely

x	y	z	t
0.1	0.9	0.8	0.8
0.1	0.1	0.8	0.8
0.2	0.6	0.3	0.3
0.5	0.7	0.1	0.5
0.9	0.1	0.1	0.1
1.0	0.0	1.0	1.0
0.5	0.4	0.6	0.6

Figure 7.9 *t represents our belief in T, where T = (X AND Y) OR Z.*
This table shows the computed values for t
given our belief in X, Y and Z.

defines high; some values are more indicative of high than
others. Figure 7.10 shows possible, but subjective, definitions
of high, medium and low. So:

Mhigh   =   0.3/0.7 + 0.9/0.9 + 1/1
Mmedium =   0.6/0.3 + 1/0.5 + 0.6/0.7
Mlow   =   1/0 + 0.9/0.1 + 0.3/0.3

If a membership value is given by the numerical value of 0.7
then this is not classed as low because its membership in
Mlow is zero. However, it has a membership value of 0.6
in the set Mmedium, and 0.3 in the set Mhigh. So a value of
0.7 could mean high, but is more indicative of medium
according to these definitions. This primary fuzzy set can be
extended to define terms like very high, not very high, high
or medium.

    Fuzzy logic can be extended to cope with rules and
inference. The results have to be interpreted and, as stated
earlier, this is subject to debate. Nevertheless, the methods
of fuzzy set theory and logic have been used successfully in
pattern-matching and cluster analysis. The enthusiasts of
fuzzy logic have used it to make rigorous models of many
methods and techniques which otherwise appear vague and
imprecise.

Other forms of logic

The types of reasoning described here are not exhaustive.
Other logics have been developed (Quine 1972); for instance,
temporal logic is used to argue about time, and modal logic

106

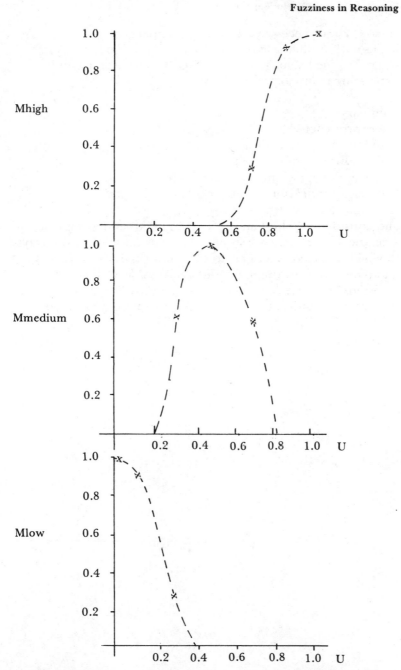

Figure 7.10 *The terms high, medium and low can be represented by fuzzy sets. These graphs show some possible definitions.*

reasons about necessity. A coherent expert can use these logics without being aware of their strict definitions. A logic programming language such as PROLOG is a useful tool for expressing many logical concepts.

Summary
There are strict logical definitions of IF . . . THEN rules based on A => B. Logical reasoning is based on these rules and modifications of them. It should therefore be possible to break down rational argument into the forms described here, e.g. implication, symptoms, analogies and incompatibilities. People reason with words, not numbers, and consider certainty and risk when making judgements. The knowledge engineer should take careful note of the ways in which the expert weighs up different types of evidence, and record the reasoning behind decisions as well as the decisions themselves. Models for dealing with uncertainty include probability, fuzzy logic and reasoning with words.

CHAPTER 8
Machine induction

Principles of induction
Most authorities acknowledge that knowledge elicitation is
a problem, but there is some controversy over the role of
machine induction. Whereas some authorities dismiss the
methods as almost worthless, others (Michie & Johnston
1985) make optimistic claims and suggest that inductive
systems may, in the future, be useful sources of knowledge.
This chapter describes induction and its potential usefulness
to the knowledge engineer.

In deduction we are given rules or facts and we then
make deductions. For example, if we are told that:

All children start school as soon as possible after their seventh birthday.

then if we know that:

Sally is at school.

we can deduce that:

Sally is at least seven years old.

If we are told that:

David is five years old.

then we deduce that:

David is not at school.

If the rule is true, and we make no false assumptions, then
the deduction will be true. The reasoning is from the general
to the specific: the rule is general, and the deduced statements
about Sally and David are specific. This is a top-down
approach.

Induction works the other way round, and is a bottom-up
method. If we do not know the rule or rules, then we need to

investigate and make sensible guesses. Given a set of examples then we induce rules which describe the examples. If the rules are good then they will apply not only to the specific examples, but also in general. Suppose we were given the following table about children:

name	age	at school?
Danny	8	yes
Sally	10	yes
David	5	no
Brian	9	yes
Jane	2	no
Ian	3	no
James	14	yes

we might induce the rule:

If the child is at least eight years old, then he/she is at school.

Clearly, the critical age could be six, seven or eight for this set of examples. The uncertainty in the induced rule is caused by the incompleteness of the example set: we have no data about children aged six or seven. Even if we did, this would not guarantee that the correct rule was induced. A child aged seven might be at school, or about to start, depending when the seventh birthday was. So the induced rules are not necessarily 'right'. However, computers can easily deal with logic, and some experts find it easier to give specific examples, rather than to talk about general principles or rules, so the basis of induction is good.

Requirements for induction
In order to be able to use induction we require the following:

Examples — the examples or *training set* form the basis of the induction process. An incomplete or inadequate set of examples is likely to result in poor rules. In the problem discussed above the training set is the set of data about children.

Attributes — The examples have sets of characteristics which describe them, and enable comparisons to be made between different examples. Some of these characteristics form the factors which influence the rules. These characteristics can be:

descriptive categories, e.g. small, medium, large
real measurements, e.g. height in metres
integer values, e.g. age in years
logical descriptions, e.g. true, false; behind, on top of.

For example, in medical diagnosis the attributes would be symptoms; in the selection of personnel for interview the attributes would be details from an application form.

Classes — The classes represent the decision or classification by the expert, e.g. yes, the patient does have the disease; or, reject this application.

Inductive algorithm — The algorithm is the method which the computer program uses to induce rules from the training set (Cohen & Feigenbaum 1982; Michie *et al.* 1977). It will depend on the form of the examples and the required output.

The quality of the induced results depends on all of these components. In other words, the induced results will be good only if a good algorithm is used on a training set which contains adequate information, in a suitable form, about the problem. If the examples do not contain certain information, or do not have a suitable representation of that information, then it may not be possible to use the algorithm to express concepts in a sensible way. To use the algorithm it must be possible to express and manipulate all the necessary concepts in the input and output. The training set must be rich enough to contain enough examples with sufficient descriptors to be able to induce these concepts. Algorithms vary in the way in which they search the training set, the way in which they generalize, and the way in which they cope with errors and signal noise in the input. Some algorithms have been designed to cope with specific types of domain knowledge, whereas others are intended to be general. The general ones tend to be less efficient and produce results which are less spectacular. The overall problem is that the knowledge engineer does not know in advance whether his training set or algorithm is good enough: to be sure of this would presuppose that he had some idea of the 'solution'; the reason for using induction in the first instance is that he does not know, but wants to discover.

There have been a number of successes with machines

learning from examples. A famous example is the work of Michalski and Chilausky (see Michie & Johnston 1985; Cohen & Feigenbaum 1982). They studied soybean diseases on a farm in Illinois, and produced two sets of rules for diagnosis. The first set was that obtained directly from the expert, and the other was induced from examples. The training set of examples consisted of the descriptions of the plants, e.g. environment, condition of leaves, condition of roots, and the expert's diagnosis. The induced rules behaved much more efficiently than the expert when presented with new examples — the machine's rules are used now! (see Michie *et al.* 1977). Their inductive algorithm was based on AQ11: there are other products on the market similar to this. The expert system AM (Automated Mathematician) has been used to research mathematical theorems and number theory. This involves the determination of more than simple rules. The successor to AM is Eurisko, which is an attempt to discover heuristics. Note that this is discovery in a very specific domain.

Computers are objective, without preconceived ideas. In the same way that children find it difficult to discover and describe patterns, experts cannot always see a simple pattern or principle, and suggest overly complex rules, when they describe what they think they ought to do, rather than what they actually do. Research in rule-devising has shown that a computer program can induce neater and simpler rules than people can.

Consider the two classes of shapes in Figure 8.1. Can you devise the simplest rule to distinguish between those in class 1 and those in class 2? When this problem was presented to a group, suggested solutions were:

If the shape contains a small dark shape it is class 1.
If there are five boxes, or a small dark circle it is class 1.
If there is a star above a triangle it is class 1.
If there is a star and it is not at the top it is class 1.
If there are two boxes or a moon shape it is class 2.
If there is a light circle or a light moon it is class 2.
If there is a large triangle at the bottom it is class 1.

There are other possible solutions. Notice that some of these proposed rules are more complex than others; there is no 'obvious' solution.

For modest projects a knowledge engineer is unlikely to

class 1

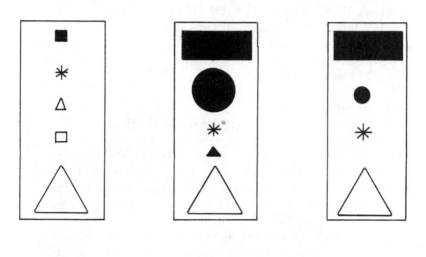

class 2

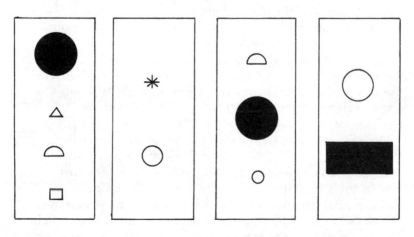

Figure 8.1 *Induction looks for generalized descriptions from the examples provided. Here we are looking for rules to distinguish shapes in class 1 from those in class 2.*

want to develop his own inductive system, and will use software which is commercially available. One algorithm which has been implemented in inductive aids and expert system shells is one developed by Ross Quinlan, called the Iterative Dichotomiser 3, or ID3 (Michie 1979). Implementations vary, and the initial algorithm has now been modified, but the underlying principles remain the same. The rest of this chapter describes the ways in which an algorithm like ID3 can be used.

ID3 rule induction

ID3 uses a training set of examples to induce IF . .. THEN . . . rules which form a simple decision tree. The examples are described by attributes and resulting classes. The original program was used to classify moves in a game of chess, and the attributes were categorical, i.e. for each attribute there was a finite set of discrete values. The classes were categorical too: either pass or fail. Most implementations now allow more than two classes, and also integer or real attributes. Ideally, the training set should contain one of each of the different types of cases which the expert has to deal with. The principles of the method are shown in Figure 8.2. The knowledge engineer draws up a training set of examples which describe the problem. This is analysed by the computer program which produces induced rules. These induced results describe the training set: they can then be used to predict results for examples not in the training set, or can be presented to the expert as a possible representation of his rules.

As has been said, the quality of the training set affects the quality of the induced rules; the algorithm cannot be used to discover something which is not there. For this reason the selection of attributes and examples is a fundamental part of the inductive process. The selection of attributes must be based on the accumulated knowledge and experience of the expert; it is not a haphazard process.

The attributes are the factors which influence the classification or decision. As shown in Figure 8.2, each rule is derived from one attribute and forms an intermediate node in the tree. The attributes should be those which seem 'natural' to the expert. The terminal nodes are the classes or decisions. Given a subset of examples ID3 selects

114

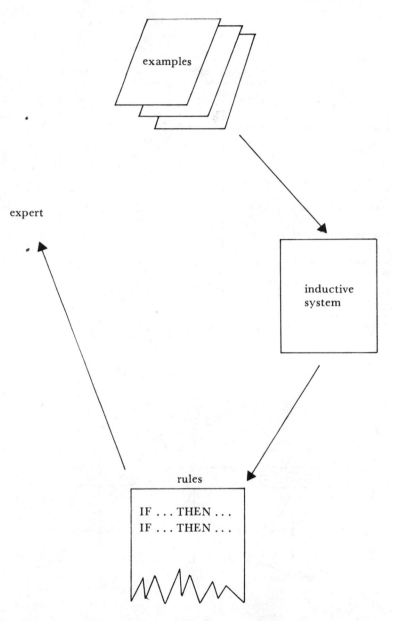

Figure 8.2 *The principles of induction: the expert draws up a set of examples; the inductive system reads these and analyses them, producing rules which describe the patterns in the examples. These induced results are then examined by the expert who may wish to modify the examples and repeat the procedure.*

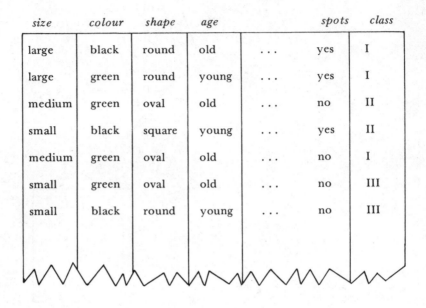

size	colour	shape	age		spots	class
large	black	round	old	. . .	yes	I
large	green	round	young	. . .	yes	I
medium	green	oval	old	. . .	no	II
small	black	square	young	. . .	yes	II
medium	green	oval	old	. . .	no	I
small	green	oval	old	. . .	no	III
small	black	round	young	. . .	no	III

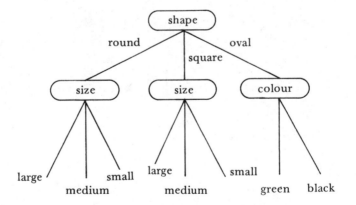

Figure 8.3 *The induction algorithm uses the information in the training set of examples. Here the induced rules are derived directly from the attributes in the training set. The way in which the examples are described is therefore very important; if the attributes are not thought out properly then the rules might be inefficient.*

the attribute which subdivides those examples in the 'best' way. A categorical attribute with N possible values will subdivide the examples into N sets. It will be the best attribute for the next rule if each of the N sets has only one type of class in it; it will be a poor attribute to select if the classes are randomly mixed between the subsets. This is illustrated in Figure 8.3. For real or integer attributes a cut-off point needs to be chosen (in an optimal way) to subdivide the examples into subsets, e.g. height > 51.2 will subdivide examples into two groups. In order to measure the degree of mixture, ID3 uses a measure of information, based on *Shannon's information statistic*. ID3 selects the attribute which results in the largest decrease in information in the example subsets. Sample values are shown in Figure 8.4 for the training set shown below:

height	colour	size	class
11.3	red	big	1
9.8	red	big	2
7.3	green	small	2
12.4	green	big	1
6.8	green	small	2
10.3	green	big	1
8.5	red	small	2
9.9	red	big	2

If the attributes are exhausted before the tree is complete then there are contradictory examples in the training set, i.e. examples with the same attribute values, but different classes. The original algorithm is not designed to cater for this, and it is sometimes necessary to introduce an extra attribute to distinguish between clashing examples.

A simple case study

The Examination Committee for a course meets to discuss the students' results. There are three courses of action: students can pass, resit or fail. Such meetings often take a long time, and so the expert adviser, who has had extensive experience of such decision-making, has been asked to draw up guidelines. The expert draws up a training set of typical cases of decisions. The classes are pass P, resit R, and fail F. Attributes are:

Altogether: three class 1 } total information = 0.95
              five class 2 }

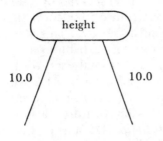

three class 1   five class 2

Information given:
height = 0
decrease = 0.95

red   green

one class 1   two class 1
three class 2   two class 2

Information given:
colour = 0.91
decrease = 0.04

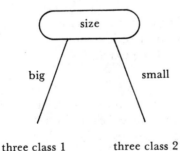

big   small

three class 1   three class 2
two class 2

Information given:
size = 0.61
decrease = 0.34

Figure 8.4 *Using the information statistic we can induce rules to describe classes. Here height gives the best rule; size is quite good, but colour is very poor.*

NFAILS — the number of failed examinations
NMARG — the number of marginal failures
ATT   — the attendance record of the student
EXT   — extenuating circumstances, e.g. illness to explain an
          unexpected failure
ANT   — the anticipated result

	NFAILS	NMARG	ATT	EXT	ANT	result
1	0	0	good	no	P	P
2	0	0	poor	yes	F	P
3	0	0	good	yes	F	P
4	3	0	good	no	F	F
5	3	1	poor	no	F	F
6	3	0	good	no	P	F
7	3	2	good	yes	P	R
8	2	1	poor	no	F	R
9	2	2	good	yes	P	R
10	1	0	poor	yes	P	R
11	1	1	good	yes	F	R
12	1	1	poor	no	F	R
13	1	0	poor	no	F	F

The induced tree is shown in Figure 8.5. After inspection of
the induced rules, the expert decided to add examples to the
training set, because he felt that the rules for two or three
failures were inadequate. He also decided to modify
example 8. The changes were:

	NFAILS	NMARG	ATT	EXT	ANT	result
8	2	1	poor	no	F	F
14	3	2	good	no	P	F
15	2	2	good	no	F	R
16	2	1	good	yes	P	R
17	2	0	poor	no	F	F

The new induced rules are shown in Figure 8.6. This time the
expert was happy to make a change to the decision tree, and
his final results are shown in Figure 8.7. The expert's
comments were:

'Many members argue about attendance records and expected results of
the candidates. These seem to be unimportant compared with the other
factors. I think the final tree sums it all up, and is a fair approximation
to what happens. I could have put more examples in, but I don't think
that would clarify the situation. The rules seem cold and clinical, but

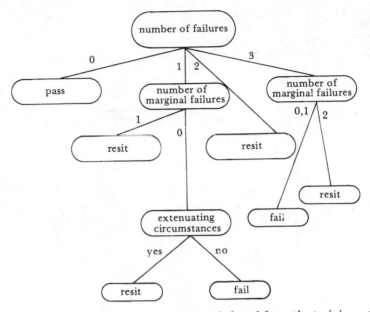

Figure 8.5 *This is the first decision tree induced from the training set drawn up by the Examinations Officer. After examining the tree the examiner felt it necessary to modify the training set.*

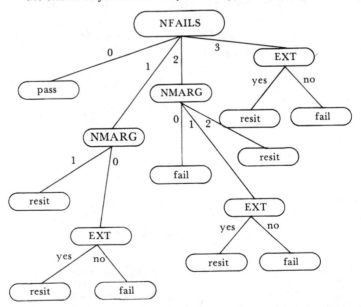

Figure 8.6 *After modifying the training set the examiner re-induced the rules. This is the second tree in this case study.*

120

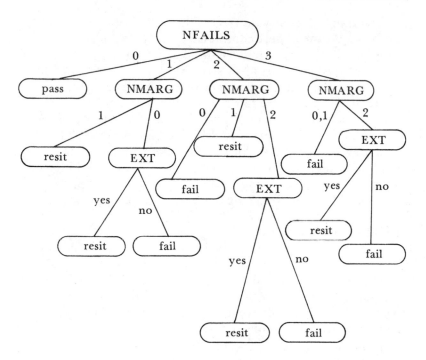

Figure 8.7 *When the examiner saw the decision tree shown in Figure 8.6 he felt that he could draw up a suitable set of rules. This tree is based on Figure 8.6 and includes a modification which the examiner introduced himself. Induction had helped to identify the overall structure of the decision-making (this example is illustrative and is not intended to describe fully any particular examination regulations).*

they do show what we usually do — all the other things are used to justify the decisions and make people feel better about it. If this was used as a guideline it would help everybody. We spend a long time arguing over a few apparently awkward cases. If the tree is right, then they needn't be awkward any more.

The skill in induction lies in the selection of examples and attributes. It is very likely that the program will be used several times, with successively refined example sets, until the output is satisfactory. In the Examinations Committee example the expert added examples, and changed another. Sometimes it is advantageous to alter the attributes too. However, care must be taken not to impose a preconceived solution on the problem.

The training set should cover all possible types of relevant problem. As the expert commented, the distribution of examples in the training set will be different from that in real life. Most students are a straightforward pass or fail, and in practice the argument concerns the borderline cases of students who might be referred. In the training set there are several examples covering these difficult cases: this is where the skill lies. The expert was able to compile this set of examples because of his knowledge about the problem. A random sample of student cases from any year would have been inadequate, as it would have described a small percentage of these difficult cases. This is a very important principle.

Results from taxonomy

Taxonomists use cluster analysis to classify objects and organisms. The process is very similar to induction; they refer to characteristics instead of attributes. There is a wealth of documented advice on the selection of characteristics (Van Ryzin 1977; Sneath & Sokal 1973), and the following guidelines should be considered:

1) Avoid characteristics which are like labels. They will describe the examples very well, but have little to do with classification. They might therefore appear in the rules, but be useless for prediction.
2) Avoid characteristics which are redundant: choose relevant and homologous attributes. Avoid adding more attributes in the hope that this will necessarily make the results better; a small, good set of descriptors is better than a large, badly thought-out set.
3) Grouping of characteristics can have an important effect on the results.
4) Beware of correlated characteristics — correlation can be statistical, functional or logical — where possible group correlated characteristics which describe different features.

These are some of the reasons why it is the expert's choice of attributes which is important. The effect of joint attributes is shown in Figure 8.8, which is a deliberately contrived example. The problem is to describe the shapes within circles. Attributes are shape, colour, X value and Y value. The simplest rule for this is DARK AND TRIANGLE. However, because ID3 selects one attribute at a time then the induced rule is $(X > 2.0)$ AND $(Y > 3.0)$ AND DARK, i.e. it selects attribute X, then attribute Y and then attribute colour. In this case the resulting rule might appear obscure or alien

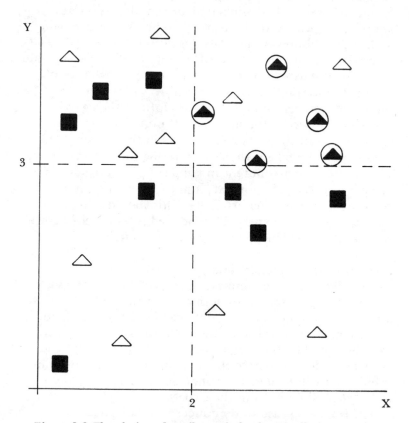

Figure 8.8 *The choice of attributes is fundamentally important.*
This example shows how the selection of attributes
can influence the induced rules. The simplest description of the
circled objects is DARK AND TRIANGLE. Rules induced
by selecting one attribute at a time could give
(X > 2.0) AND (Y > 3.0) AND DARK. It is the grouping of attributes
and the choice of relevant attributes that requires the expertise
of the expert.

to the expert. If the expert describes an attribute as 'dark
and triangle' then it should be kept as a joint attribute, and
not separated into the two attributes, dark-light and
triangle-square.

The rules should always be inspected carefully. If possible
they should be tested on examples which are not in the
training set. Their power is not in the ability to classify

examples in the training set, but in their predictive power for further examples. The original algorithm did this, but many implementations leave the testing to the user. A problem with real attributes is that they result in rules like $X > 10.6$, where 10.6 is an induced cut-off point. These rules and values should be discussed carefully with the expert who should be able to interpret the value 10.6 if it is meaningful. Inductive systems would be more helpful if they gave confidence intervals for such cut-off points, because they can be very sensitive to small changes in the training set.

Care must be taken when interpreting the induced rules. The fact that an attribute is missing from the tree does not mean that it is not important; it might mean that it is correlated with another attribute. This should also be discussed with the expert. The induced rules do not describe confirmatory evidence, only necessary evidence.

Problems with uncertain data

The original ID3 algorithm assumes that the examples are complete and correct. In practice the examples can be difficult to procure, and the data can be incomplete and uncertain. When this is the case the results need very careful examination. Medical diagnosis is a typical example of a knowledge domain where the data are uncertain, and the training set will be derived from case histories or experiment rather than directly from the expert.

The following case study concerns the diagnosis of gallstones, based on various symptoms in the patients' case notes. The attributes are all categorical.

sex	age	time	SEV	RAD	HYP	ATT	gallstones
F	old	long	N	N	Y	Y	Y
F	old	long	Y	SH	N	Y	Y
F	old	short	N	N	Y	Y	Y
F	old	short	Y	Y	Y	Y	Y
M	old	long	Y	N	Y	Y	Y
F	old	long	N	Y	N	Y	Y
F	old	short	N	N	Y	N	Y
F	old	long	Y	SH	N	N	Y
F	old	short	Y	N	N	Y	Y
M	old	medium	Y	SH	Y	Y	Y
F	old	medium	Y	Y	Y	Y	Y
F	old	medium	N	N	N	Y	Y

sex	age	time	SEV	RAD	HYP	ATT	gallstones
F	old	long	Y	N	Y	N	Y
F	old	short	Y	N	N	Y	Y
F	young	short	Y	Y	N	Y	Y
F	old	medium	Y	Y	Y	Y	Y
F	young	short	Y	SH	Y	N	Y
F	old	medium	Y	SH	N	Y	Y
M	old	long	N	Y	Y	Y	N
F	young	long	N	N	N	Y	N
F	old	long	Y	N	N	N	N
M	old	short	Y	Y	N	N	N
F	old	short	N	N	N	N	N
M	old	long	Y	N	N	N	N
M	young	medium	Y	N	N	N	N
F	young	long	Y	N	N	Y	N
M	young	short	N	Y	N	N	N
F	old	long	N	N	N	N	N
M	young	short	N	N	N	N	N
F	old	long	N	N	Y	Y	N
M	old	long	N	N	Y	N	N
M	old	long	N	N	N	N	N
F	old	short	N	N	N	N	N
F	young	long	N	N	N	N	N
F	old	short	N	N	Y	N	N
F	young	long	N	N	N	N	N
F	old	short	N	Y	N	N	N
M	old	long	N	Y	N	N	N
F	old	long	N	N	Y	N	N
M	old	medium	N	SH	Y	N	N
F	old	short	N	N	N	N	N
F	old	long	N	N	N	N	N
M	old	medium	N	N	N	N	N
M	old	short	Y	Y	N	N	N
F	old	short	N	N	N	N	N
F	old	long	Y	N	N	N	N
M	young	medium	Y	N	N	N	N
F	young	long	Y	N	N	Y	N
M	young	short	N	Y	N	N	N
F	young	long	Y	N	N	N	N

Key:

sex   — male or female
age   — recorded as young or old
time   — the length of time for which the symptoms have been
            present; recorded as short, medium or long
SEV   — a logical variable denoting whether or not pain was
            severe enough to warrant emergency help
RAD   — an indication of whether pain radiated, and if so as far
            as the shoulder
HYP   — whether or not there was pain in the right hypochondrium
ATT   — whether or not there were attacks of pain.

The induced rules are shown in Figure 8.9. Also shown on the tree is the number of examples at each terminal node; this is useful information. In some cases the classification is not known, and there are clashes. This also illustrates a further problem. Some of the lower nodes on the tree add very little to the accuracy of the prediction. This is a possible problem with induced trees; the lower parts of the tree are likely to be very sensitive to small changes in the training set, i.e. the evidence for them is weak. The theory that a bigger tree is better is not always true.

Very important work has been done in this area by statisticians (Breiman, Friedman, Olshen & Stone 1984). Their results show that the best solution seems to be first growing the tree completely and then pruning it back. Pruning consists of weighing up the cost of a more complex tree against the risk of misclassification, and identifies weak links in the tree. It is more efficient to prune a tree than to stop it growing to completion. The disadvantage of stopping a tree growing is illustrated in Figure 8.10. Pruning allows one branch from a node to remain and another to disappear, whereas stopping growth would remove both branches.

If the tree is to be used for prediction, as is the case in expert system applications, then it is essential that the results are verified and the misclassification rate estimated by testing it on examples other than the training set. If there are insufficient examples to be divided into a training set and test set, then the set can be divided into n subsets — the tree grown on (n − 1) of them and tested on the nth, and this repeated for each of the other subsets. (This is described fully in an excellent book on classification and regression trees — see bibliography.) [Success rate is that for different types of cases.] For example, if 75 per cent of the cases a doctor deals with are influenza then a one-rule system would have a success rate of at least 75 per cent, but would contain no expertise. The expertise lies in being able to deal with uncommon and difficult cases as well.

General comments
Experts find it easier to describe examples and attributes than decision-making processes. Induction is objective, consistent and indefatigable, although its reasoning powers are limited. It can be used to discover knowledge and identify

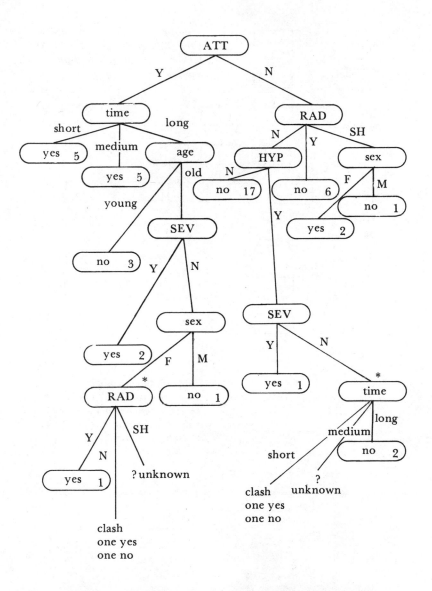

Figure 8.9 *This tree represents the induced rules from the hypothetical training set of symptoms and diagnoses. Although the results adequately describe the training set there are contradictions and omissions highlighted in the tree. Certain branches on the tree, marked *, may need pruning.*

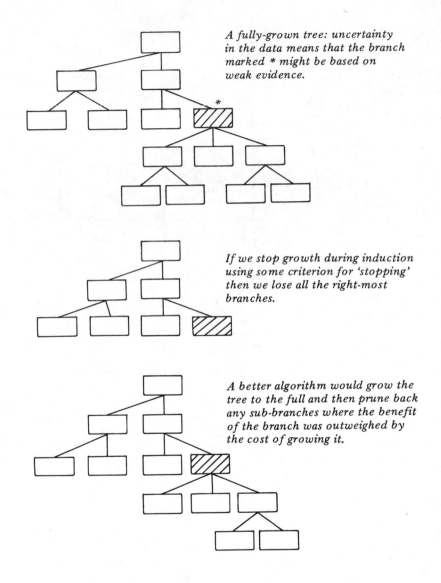

A fully-grown tree: uncertainty in the data means that the branch marked * might be based on weak evidence.

If we stop growth during induction using some criterion for 'stopping' then we lose all the right-most branches.

A better algorithm would grow the tree to the full and then prune back any sub-branches where the benefit of the branch was outweighed by the cost of growing it.

Figure 8.10 *When data are uncertain then the accuracy of lower parts of the tree needs investigation. Growing a tree to the full and then pruning it back usually gives better results than stopping growth during induction.*

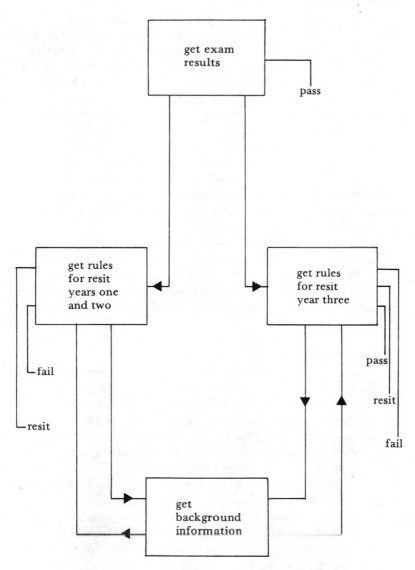

Figure 8.11 *If the problem can be structured into sub-problems then this should be reflected in the knowledge. Some inductive systems allow the user to structure the training set into subsets to match the problem. If this is not possible then the knowledge engineer may wish to use inductive methods on small problems and then link them together.*
This is a much better approach than constructing one very large training set where some attribute values may be known to be irrelevant.

129

gaps, contradictions, interesting or difficult cases, and straightforward rules. It cannot replace an interview with an expert, who should always advise on the choice of examples and attributes, and interpret results. The training set may need refining several times. Some inductive systems have their own program to select a training set. Others leave this to the knowledge engineer [and some documentation is inadequate in this respect].

For uncertain data the lower parts of the tree may be misleading, but the method makes few assumptions about statistical distributions, and unlike many statistical techniques, the output is easy to understand. In general, uncertainty in the classes is much more serious than uncertainty in the attribute values.

The inductive aids would be more useful if they gave more information about the output, e.g. the number of examples at a node, indications of where the choice between attributes was arbitrary, etc. The ability to justify and explain results should be a feature of inductive aids as it is of a good expert system.

The structured approach

We have stressed the advisability of breaking down large problems into smaller ones. The same principle should be applied to inductive methods. In a structured approach to induction we should identify sub-problems with their attributes and training sets, and build these into a solution. Figure 8.11 shows a possible structure for dealing with examination results for three years of a course. The referral rules are different in year three because it is possible to pass without actually meeting all the requirements. The background information is the same for each year. This is a better approach than building up a very large training set which would include redundant attribute values for certain examples.

Summary

The principle of induction, where a program learns general rules or descriptions from a set of specific examples, is good. However, the quality of the induced results depends on the quality of the training set, and it is essential that the training examples are drawn up by the expert in the form which seems most natural to him. The output should be tested for its predictive powers on examples other than those used to grow the decision tree. The output can be used to provoke discussion, and is useful to highlight difficult or interesting problems, as well as to suggest rules.

CHAPTER 9

The repertory grid

Personal construct theory
The psychologist Kelly (1955) developed a model of human
thinking called *personal construct theory*. According to this
theory each person is a scientist with his own personal model
of the world about him. This scientist classifies and
categorizes about his world, developing theories about it.
Based on these theories he is able to anticipate, and then act
on the basis of his anticipations.

This model matches our view of an expert at work: it is a
description of the development and use of his knowledge.
The *repertory grid technique* is a method of eliciting and
analysing such a model, and is therefore a tool which can
be useful in knowledge elicitation. The method has its
critics; the main objection is that, owing to the very nature
of the theory, the results will be personal, i.e. very subjective.
Two experts addressing the same problem can produce quite
different sets of results. However, this characteristic can be
exploited. There is evidence (Newell & Simon 1972) that it
is the way in which experts see problems which distinguishes
them from novices. Research in physics showed that while
novices described problems by their surface characteristics
experts classified them according to a law of physics
appropriate for their solution. In this way the method of
classification actually constitutes part of the expertise of the
expert; examples are given below:

Novice: This is a block on a slope.
Expert: This is Newton's second law.

Novice: My program does not read all of the numbers from the file.
Expert: The controlling loop structure of the program is wrong.

Novice: The plumber is trying to charge me more than he said, and
caused damage while doing the job.

Expert: The issue is whether the price he gave you was an estimate or a quotation for the job.

The expert does not simply identify a cause which explains an effect: he sees the problem in a particular way. Knowledge elicitation is the process of defining these underlying principles, categories and theories, so that a computer can mimic the expert at work.

The grid

The repertory grid is a representation of the expert's view of a particular problem. A grid is composed of constructs and elements. These are similar to the attributes and examples described for induction. A *construct* is a bipolar characteristic which each element has to some degree. Examples of constructs are friendly-unfriendly, heavy-light, brave-cowardly, large-small. 'Shape' cannot be a construct because there are many ways of defining it. In order to include characteristics associated with shape it would be necessary to define specific bipolar constructs, i.e. characteristics which can be represented by a rating along a linear scale. If curvature were one of these then a suitable construct could be straight-curved. Using this construct, circles and spheres would be rated highly whereas lines and cubes would be given a low rating.

As the expert selects the constructs he must understand what makes a valid construct, and how it is used. Sometimes, to help the expert, ratings are described by names rather than numbers, although subsequent analysis normally uses numerical values, e.g. on a scale of 1 to 5 with a construct heavy-light suitable descriptions could be:

1 very heavy
2 heavy
3 medium weight
4 light
5 very light

It is important that the scale must be the same throughout the grid (i.e. 1 to 3 or 1 to 5) although the terms used to describe particular ratings might vary from construct to construct.

Each *element* is rated according to each construct, using a subjective rating supplied by the expert. This rating enables elements to be ranked or compared. For example, suppose

134

the construct is friendly-unfriendly on a scale of 1 to 5.
If Susan is rated as 4, Fred as 2, and Bill as 3 then this means
that Fred is most friendly, then Bill, then Susan. However,
it does not imply that Fred is twice as friendly as Susan.
We have already met these ideas of subjective rankings:
they are similar to membership values in fuzzy logic. This is
illustrated in Figure 9.1.

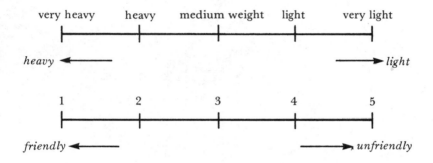

Figure 9.1 *Bipolar constructs allow subjective ratings of elements;*
they facilitate comparison and ranking
although they may not be measurements.

The elements are key examples, produced by the expert, and
described by the values of the constructs. For example,
when investigating symptoms of a disease the elements
would be patient case notes. In fault diagnosis the elements
would be examples of faulty and perfect items from a
production line. The grid is a cross-referencing system
between the elements and constructs. It is similar to the
training set used in induction with elements for examples
and constructs for attributes, but there are fewer restrictions
on attributes than on constructs.

The repertory grid is useful to the expert or knowledge
engineer for two reasons:

1) The elicitation of a grid makes the expert think twice about a
   problem, and helps clarify issues in his mind.
2) Grids can be analysed to find patterns or associations for
   further investigation. This is normally at an overview or
   concept level — large grids describing great detail tend to be
   unmanageable.

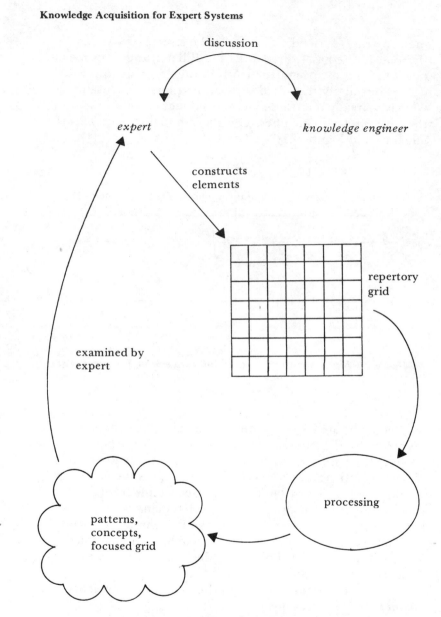

Figure 9.2 *The expert draws up a repertory grid to show his perception of a problem. The knowledge engineer may assist him in this. The grid is analysed to find patterns or associations and general concepts. After examining this the expert may wish to change his grid. The method is useful in the early stages of knowledge elicitation, especially if the expert finds it difficult to verbalize his thoughts.*

Figure 9.2 shows how a grid can be used by an expert. The grid is most useful in the early stages of elicitation, as a means of encouraging an expert to describe concepts and principles. Once this has been done then other methods can be used to elicit details.

Grid elicitation

Before drawing up a grid it is important to define the problem under investigation. The expert or eliciter must state a clear objective for his analysis (Shaw & McKnight 1981). Suitable problems could be: the classification of skin diseases, evaluation of candidates for a job, or features of well-designed bridges. These problems should be specific rather than general. A more general problem, and one more difficult to define, would be one such as features of good design, or the classification of diseases.

Having defined his objective the expert sets about the task of drawing up the grid. If he can write down the elements and constructs straight away then the grid can be analysed. However, in most cases the elicitation is not trivial and involves repeated comparison of elements. It is common for the expert to produce his elements first. These are then compared and contrasted in order to obtain more detail in further elements and constructs. A group of three is the smallest from which he can describe a similarity and a difference. This comparison can form the basis for a new construct. The groups of three can be chosen randomly or systematically. An example is shown below:

Knowledge engineer: Consider your elements Susan, Fred and Bill; choose the two which are most similar.

Expert: Susan and Bill are similar and different from Fred.

Knowledge engineer: What makes Susan and Bill similar?

Expert: They are both mature.

Knowledge engineer: What is the opposite of mature, which describes Fred?

Expert: He is immature.

Knowledge engineer: The poles for your construct are mature and immature. Now rank each of your elements on a 1 to 5 scale with 1 being immature and 5 mature.

By comparing different sets of constructs the expert builds up a grid describing all the elements which he considers relevant to the problem under discussion. At any stage in this process the expert can introduce new elements or constructs, remove elements or constructs, and change rating values. The process is complete when the expert is happy that the grid describes his view of the problem under investigation.

Grid analysis
Once the grid has been elicited it can be analysed. This analysis is not intended to make the expert change his mind, nor is it used to invent or misconstrue intentions (Shaw 1981). It is a way of exhibiting structure and pattern in the grid, to provide feedback to the expert. The analysis is a tool to help the expert identify a structure which he recognizes as natural. If he disagrees with the analysis then he will probably wish to alter the grid. In this way the method can assist the expert to represent his knowledge and encourage him to think and re-think his knowledge. Methods of analysis are based on statistical theory, and include *factor analysis* and *principal component analysis*. Mildred Shaw, who has done much to make the technique easy to use in business and industrial applications, has used a simple method of *cluster analysis*. In the cluster analysis, elements and constructs are compared. Cluster analysis defines a measure of difference between two objects and then groups a set of such objects into clusters; objects in the same cluster are more similar than those in other clusters. Similarity is defined by the measure of distance between the clusters. This is a simple and effective way of describing the underlying patterns. Figure 9.3 shows a typical cluster.

If two objects are similar then they are correlated in some way. Cluster analysis is a technique which is used frequently in taxonomy. The results of the grid analysis enable attributes and elements to be re-ordered so that similar objects appear near to each other in a focused grid. The expert may wish to investigate the problem further on the basis of this focused grid. The method is best illustrated by example, and the rest of this chapter describes a case study.

A case study in repertory grid
The following is a transcript of a dialogue between a knowledge engineer (K) and an expert (E):

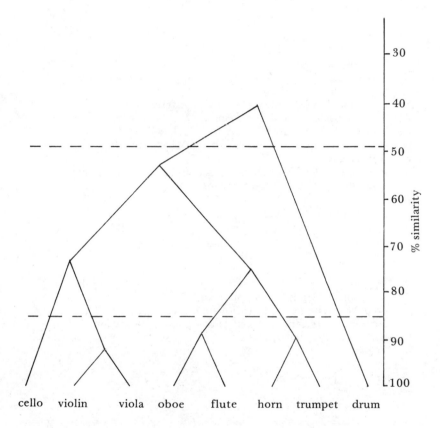

Figure 9.3 *Clustering: this cluster shows the relationships between musical instruments, e.g. violin and viola are most similar, a drum is not very like any of the others. The cluster enables the entities to be grouped depending on the level of similarity required. At a level of 85% there would be five groups; at a level of 50% there would be two groups.*

K: Please state the problem you wish to investigate.

E: I am going to look at different students on our course, because I am interested in our selection procedure.

K: Please supply your elements — examples of students who you think are important in this investigation.

E: They are —

1) Brian
2) Kim
3) Terry
4) Ian
5) Stephen
6) Nadia

K: From Brian, Kim and Terry select two who are similar and different from the third.

E: Brian and Terry are similar — Kim is different.

K: What makes Brian and Terry similar?

E: They are both mature.

K: Mature is one pole of your construct. What is the other pole?

E: School-leaver.

K: Now rate each of your elements according to this construct where 1 means school-leaver and 3 means mature.

E: They are —

1) Brian 3
2) Kim 1
3) Terry 3
4) Ian 1
5) Stephen 1
6) Nadia 1

K: Your next group is Ian, Stephen and Nadia.

E: Stephen has better qualifications than Nadia and Ian. The poles are poor qualifications (rated 1) and good qualifications (rated 3). My elements are —

1) Brian 1
2) Kim 2
3) Terry 1
4) Ian 2
5) Stephen 3
6) Nadia 2

K: Your next group is Brian, Terry and Stephen.

E: Brian and Stephen are both self-confident; Terry is not. My poles are unsure (rated 1) and self-confident (rated 3). The ratings are —

1) Brian 3
2) Kim 1
3) Terry 1
4) Ian 2
5) Stephen 3
6) Nadia 1

K: The next group is Kim, Ian and Nadia.

E: Kim and Nadia do not ask questions in class; Ian does. My poles will be asks questions (rated 1) and quiet (rated 3).

1) Brian 1
2) Kim 3
3) Terry 2
4) Ian 3
5) Stephen 1
6) Nadia 3

I think I will change the rating for Ian to 2.

K: Do you want to choose your own group?
E: Yes: Brian, Ian and Kim. Brian and Ian are good attenders; Kim is not. My poles are good attender (rated 1) and poor attender (rated 3).

1) Brian 1
2) Kim 3
3) Terry 3
4) Ian 1
5) Stephen 2
6) Nadia 2.

I shall choose another triad: Ian, Stephen and Kim. Ian and Stephen do the set work; Kim does not. My poles are does work (rated 1), does not do work (rated 3).

1) Brian 1
2) Kim 3
3) Terry 2
4) Ian 1
5) Stephen 1
6) Nadia 3

I shall add another element: David. His ratings are —
school-leaver/mature 1
poor qualifications/good qualifications 2
unsure/self-confident 3
asks questions/quiet 2
good attender/poor attender 3
does work/does not do work 1

I want to add more constructs. They are —
joins in socially/does not join in socially
is not organized/is organized
scruffy/tidy

The ratings are —

1) Brian   1 3 3
2) Kim   3 1 1
3) Terry   3 1 1
4) Ian   2 2 2
5) Stephen 2 3 3
6) Nadia   3 2 3
7) David   1 1 1

I think that is all I need.

		E1	E2	E3	E4	E5	E6	E7		
	Comparison of students on a course									
C1	school-leaver	3	1	3	1	1	1	1	mature	C1
C2	poor qualifications	1	2	1	2	3	2	2	good qualifications	C2
C3	unsure	3	1	1	2	3	1	3	confident	C3
C4	asks questions	1	3	2	2	1	3	2	quiet	C4
C5	good attendance	1	3	3	1	2	2	3	poor attendance	C5
C6	does work	1	3	2	1	1	3	1	does not work	C6
C7	joins in socially	1	3	3	2	2	3	1	does not join in	C7
C8	not organized	3	1	1	2	3	2	1	organized	C8
C9	scruffy	3	1	1	2	3	3	1	tidy	C9

Brian

Kim

Terry

Ian

Stephen

Nadia

David

(removed)

Figure 9.4 *A repertory grid*
drawn up by an expert considering different types of students on a course.

	E1	E2	E3	E4	E5	E6	E7
E1	—	15	10	7	6	13	8
E2		—	5	8	11	2	7
E3			—	9	12	7	8
E4				—	5	6	5
E5					—	9	6
E6						—	9
E7							—

differences

	E1	E2	E3	E4	E5	E6	E7
E1	—	6	38	56	63	19	50
E2		—	69	50	31	88	56
E3			—	44	25	56	50
E4				—	69	63	69
E5					—	44	63
E6						—	44
E7							—

% similarity

Figure 9.5 *Comparison of elements: elements are compared by measuring the difference between them, and this enables measures of similarity to be computed.*

143

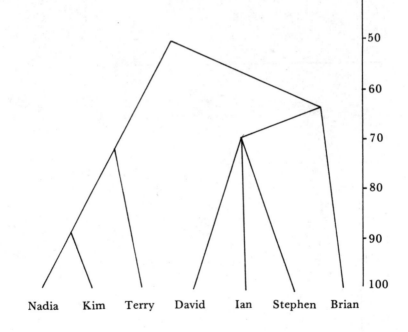

Figure 9.6 *The clusters of elements derived from the grid*
shown in Figure 9.4.

The expert's grid was drawn up, and is shown in Figure 9.4.
On seeing this the expert's comment was:

'The construct "appearance" seems very similar to "organization",
which is probably more important. I shall delete "appearance". That
seems OK now.'

USING CLUSTER ANALYSIS TO FOCUS THE GRID

In order to perform clustering we need to define a way of
measuring the distance between a pair of elements. In this
particular case (see Shaw & McKnight 1981) the distance
measure used was the sum of the absolute values of the
differences between ratings, e.g. comparing Brian and Kim:

$$3 \quad 1 \quad 3 \quad 1 \quad 1 \quad 1 \quad 1 \quad 3$$
$$1 \quad 2 \quad 1 \quad 3 \quad 3 \quad 3 \quad 3 \quad 1$$

The sum of the differences is $2 + 1 + 2 + 2 + 2 + 2 + 2 + 2 = 15$

Repeating this procedure for all pairs of elements we derive
the table shown in Figure 9.5. If dij is the difference measure
between elements i and j then their measure of similarity is:

$$\frac{-100dij}{2 \times 8} + 100$$

Note that this has the maximum value of 100 when dij = 0
and the minimum value of 0 when dij has its maximal value
of 16. The maximal value of dij is 16 because the largest
possible difference for a single construct is two (i.e. $3 - 1$)
and there are eight constructs per element. Two elements are
similar if their similarity measure is above 50, and dissimilar
if it is below 50. Their similarity is therefore measured on a
linear scale between 0 and 100. Figure 9.6 shows the clusters
derived from these measures.

The comparison of constructs is slightly more complex.
In this case it is necessary to compare reversed constructs
as well as constructs. For example, if we were comparing
physical characteristics of people, say the constructs short-
tall and heavy-light, then we would not expect a high
similarity (or correlation) between them. However, if we
reversed one of them then we might expect a similarity, e.g.
short-tall and light-heavy could be similar. Clearly, it makes
no sense to reverse ratings for particular elements. A reversed
construct X' is derived from the construct X by substituting
the opposite rating; in this case 1 to 3, 2 to 2 and 3 to 1, e.g.:

	E1	E2	E3	E4	E5	E6	E7
C1	3	1	3	1	1	1	1
C1′	1	3	1	3	3	3	3

The differences are calculated, with the lower left half of the table containing the values where one construct is reversed. In this case the measure of similarity is:

$$\frac{-200 d_{ij}}{2 \times 7} + 100$$

which will range from -100 to $+100$. The value of 100 corresponds to two constructs which are equivalent; the value of -100 describes the case where they are opposite. The values for this case study are shown in Figure 9.7.

	C1	C2	C3	C4	C5	C6	C7	C8
C1		−43	0	−29	−14	0	−14	14
C2	43		29	29	14	0	14	43
C3	0	0		−43	−29	−71	−57	57
C4	29	29	71		29	71	57	−29
C5	14	14	29	−29		29	43	−43
C6	0	0	71	−43	−29		57	−29
C7	14	14	86	−29	−14	−57		−14
C8	−14	14	−29	57	71	29	43	

Figure 9.7 *Comparison of constructs: when comparing constructs it is necessary to calculate the similarity between each pair of constructs (as for elements), but also the similarity between pairs of constructs where one construct has been reversed. The lower half of the table contains the values for these latter measures.*

Figure 9.8 shows the clusters. This indicates groups or clusters of similar constructs with a measure of that similarity.

A *focused grid* is derived by ordering the constructs and elements as indicated by the clusters, so that similar items are close together. Reversed constructs are used in the grid where appropriate. Figure 9.9 shows the focused grid.

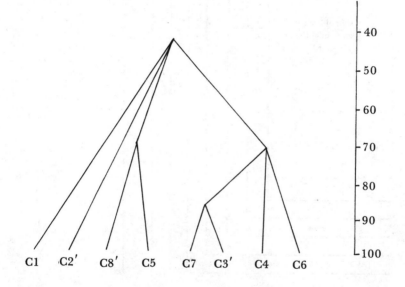

C1   C2′   C8′   C5   C7   C3′   C4   C6

40
50
60
70
80
90
100

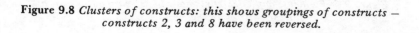

Figure 9.8 *Clusters of constructs: this shows groupings of constructs —*
constructs 2, 3 and 8 have been reversed.

147

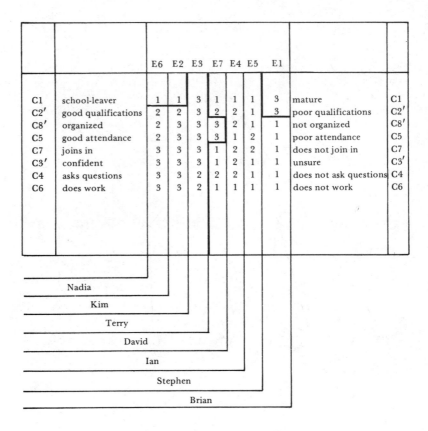

		E6	E2	E3	E7	E4	E5	E1		
C1	school-leaver	1	1	3	1	1	1	3	mature	C1
C2′	good qualifications	2	2	3	2	2	1	3	poor qualifications	C2′
C8′	organized	2	3	3	3	2	1	1	not organized	C8′
C5	good attendance	2	3	3	3	1	2	1	poor attendance	C5
C7	joins in	3	3	3	1	2	2	1	does not join in	C7
C3′	confident	3	3	3	1	2	1	1	unsure	C3′
C4	asks questions	3	3	2	2	2	1	1	does not ask questions	C4
C6	does work	3	3	2	1	1	1	1	does not work	C6

Nadia
Kim
Terry
David
Ian
Stephen
Brian

Figure 9.9 *The focused grid: this is the grid derived from that shown in Figure 9.4. Elements and constructs have been re-organized so that similar entities are near to each other.*

THE EXPERT'S REACTION

The expert's objective in exploring the grid was to look at different students on the course to review the selection procedure. His comments on the focused grid were:

'Yes, the mature students are either excellent or weak. You can't tell the difference from their applications, as they often have weak academic backgrounds. The ones who succeed, like Brian, have the determination and self-confidence. Ones like Terry give up because they feel they can't cope. Mature students need careful counselling. Stephen has a good academic background and works well — he is a 'no problem' case. Kim is just lazy and without interest; you sometimes get a clue in the reference, but his qualifications are all right. David is a gambler. He is quite bright and able to do the work, so he does not attend all the classes. It is sometimes difficult to distinguish between a David and a Kim until well into a course. Ian is a plodder. Nadia is similar to Kim but might just succeed.

Interestingly enough, my grid shows that qualifications are out on a limb. So is maturity. The point is that we would only take on poorly qualified students if they were mature. I think that the other constructs can be re-grouped into lazy-diligent and quiet-active participation. I shall include a new element — Anne. She is very quiet but diligent, and a good student. I shall also include their probable results as fail-pass. I shall change the construct school-leaver-mature to immature-mature which seems to make more sense.'

The expert altered the grid, and the two new grids are shown in Figures 9.10 and 9.11. His verdict was then:

'That's about right. The mature students are difficult. The most important thing is to join in and take part. They can get away with being quiet if they're quite bright and work very hard. Overall they need reasonable qualifications and the right attitude.'

The grid's usefulness

Grids can be analysed in more detail than this, and grids from more than one person can be compared and contrasted (Shaw 1981). This is usually done by a computer program. The grid elicitation can be part of an interactive dialogue too. Different methods can be used to perform the clustering, e.g. fuzzy logic or statistics, but the principles are the same. In some respects the analysis is similar to induction because the method involves suggesting patterns and associations between input items. However, much of the generalization in repertory grid analysis is done by the expert based on the formal analysis.

The main asset of a grid is that it makes the expert think carefully about a problem. He may want to change constructs

Second grid comparing students

	E1	E2	E3	E4	E5	E6	E7	E8		
C1 immature	3	1	1	3	1	1	2	3	mature	C1
C2 good qualifications	2	2	2	3	2	2	1	3	poor qualifications	C2
C3 diligent	1	2	3	3	3	2	1	1	lazy	C3
C4 extrovert	3	3	3	2	2	2	2	1	quiet	C4
C5 pass	2	2	3	3	1	2	1	1	fail	C5

E1 Anne
E2 Nadia
E3 Kim
E4 Terry
E5 David
E6 Ian
E7 Stephen
E8 Brian

Figure 9.10 *The second grid drawn up after the expert had examined the analysis of his first grid.*

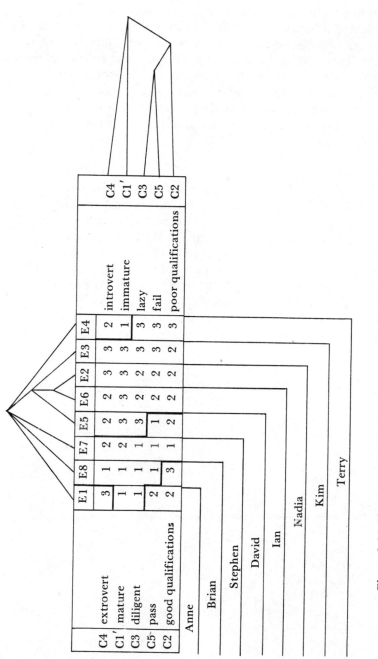

Figure 9.11 *The focused grid, showing clusters, derived from the grid shown in Figure 9.10.*

151

or elements in order to produce a grid which he likes. By producing a focused grid it is easy to see the relationships between objects, and patterns or associations emerge easily. In this sense the grid is more informative than rule induction. After drawing up the grid the expert will probably have more idea of rules, i.e. his perception may be clearer. The method can also be used to select attributes and examples for induction, or to break down a complex problem into smaller sub-problems.

Summary
The repertory grid is a technique that is often used in psychology. It is a very simple way for an expert to represent his thoughts about a specific problem. By comparing different examples he can set up a grid of elements and constructs that describe his perception of a particular problem. Cluster analysis can be used to identify patterns and associations in the grid, thereby causing the expert to focus his thoughts on key issues. It is an easy method which can be useful for eliciting general principles, or helping an expert to 'get started'.

CHAPTER 10

Try it anyway – two case studies

The process of knowledge acquisition is far from easy.
Previous chapters have outlined some of the problems which
can be encountered and described ways of tackling them.
In this chapter two case studies illustrate the ways in which
quite different projects developed. Although relatively few
projects have become famous, there are many people
reporting encouraging results from their ventures. The
process of knowledge acquisition can prove a very useful
exercise, even if it does not necessarily result in an
operational expert system.

Attersley Vegetable Research Station
Attersley Vegetable Research Station carries out research
into the production of hardy disease-free vegetables. The
centre employs many scientists including biologists,
statisticians and computer experts. This case study describes
some aspects of a project to develop an expert system.

BACKGROUND
A manager, Bill, had heard about recent developments in
artificial intelligence and reports of successful projects in
the development of expert systems. He thought that the
techniques might be useful in some of the classification work
carried out at the station. In order to investigate the
feasibility of such a project he asked for an investigation by
a programmer, Chris, and a researcher, Dave. They attended
a conference about current developments in expert systems
and asked to be put on mailing lists for further information
about publications and software tools.

On returning to Attersley they wrote a report for Bill
outlining the content of the conference, and justifying their

conclusion that AI techniques would not have any great advantage over their existing methods using cluster analysis. Some weeks later Bill received a memorandum from the chief statistician, Joe, complaining about the amount of time he spent helping researchers with statistics. After discussing the problem with Chris he arranged a meeting with Joe, Chris, Dave and himself. Chris, who had some knowledge of psychology, was confident that it would be practical and useful to develop an expert system to relieve Joe. Dave was in favour of the project, but Joe was very sceptical, although willing to help in any venture which was designed to free some of his time.

Bill decided to authorize an investigation into the possibility of an expert system. He put Chris in charge. The terms of reference were as follows:

1) The initial investigation was to take no more than two months.
2) The aim of the study was to clarify the problems experienced by Joe, and to assess the feasibility of developing an expert system.
3) The study should define a specific problem for the expert system, outlining the benefits to Joe and the station as a whole.
4) Bill would notify all relevant departments about the project and ask for their cooperation.
5) The recommendations were to be agreed by Bill, Joe and Dave before any technical work could begin.

Chris had studied statistics, and knew a little about the packages available for use on the computer. He decided to read up about the subject to refresh his memory, and become familiar with the terminology and routines. He spent about two weeks reading books and looking through the manuals in the computer centre. Having done this he felt ready to meet Joe. Arranging a meeting with Joe proved to be difficult, and Chris had the feeling that he was deliberately being awkward. This first meeting was not very productive. Joe spent most of the time complaining about the researchers' lack of statistical training.

'Nowadays I get more than one a week coming for an afternoon wasting my time. They come with half-baked ideas and expect me to solve all their problems of poor design. I shouldn't have to waste my time doing this. They're not difficult for me, though. It just takes time. They're using fairly advanced techniques. I suppose they have learnt about them, but they don't understand them — I'm their insurance policy. Biologists are always the same — they know a little about statistics, and not enough. A little knowledge is a dangerous thing. I've logged the time I spent over the past months: it's horrific. I don't even find it interesting. It's all my goodwill — I could refuse. I might soon . . .'

It was clear that little would be achieved by pressing Joe for more details. Chris thanked him for his time, sympathized with his problem and promised not to take up too much of his time. He told Joe that he would inform him of any results as soon as they were available. After this he decided to investigate the other side of the problem: the researchers in the laboratories.

THE USERS' VIEW

Chris went back to Dave and spent an afternoon discussing the problems faced by the scientists. It was difficult to describe the experiments in the office, and they arranged that Chris should spend two weeks actually in the laboratories observing the work, and asking questions of the people there. Dave explained to the staff the purpose of the investigation, and most people were happy to have Chris with them. Chris spent the time watching experiments, listening to discussions, and asking questions. He scribbled notes in a notebook, and copied them out neatly at night. At the end of this time he felt that he had some understanding of the work of the laboratories, and the types of situation which led people to consult Joe. In fact they did this reluctantly, when they felt that they could not resolve the situation without expert advice. There were other occasions when they would have liked to have talked to an expert, but did not. Almost without exception, the scientists thought that a training course would not solve the problem: what they wanted was a 'friendly expert' on call.

Chris spent the next few days reading through his notes, and making summaries and observations. He was convinced that there was a need for extra support, either another statistician or a program. On reading through Joe's comments he noticed the reference to logs. He had not realized their significance before. What he needed was some more information about the cases Joe dealt with: the logs might provide this.

BACK TO THE EXPERT

He went back to Joe and asked him about these logs. Joe had recorded the dates and duration of meetings, together with

the names of the people involved. He had not recorded
details of the actual problems. He was happy to let Chris have
a photocopy. Chris went back to the people mentioned and
asked them why they had been to Joe, and he also wrote
down a short description of each of the experiments under
discussion. Using these and his observations in the laboratories
he spent another afternoon with Dave drawing up a set of
'typical' case studies.

Chris then felt that he had enough information about the
problems to hold a fruitful meeting with Joe. Joe agreed to
spend a morning talking through the typed case studies,
and did not object to this being tape recorded. Joe was able
to give his solutions fairly quickly. His solutions consisted of
assumptions and a technique, e.g. 'I guess there's no reason
to doubt that a normal approximation won't be okay.
Anyway, the test's pretty robust. It's a bit hairy, but a
paired t-test should do. A one-sided test — you're looking
for improvement.' After he had talked through the diagnoses
Joe commented,

'You must know something about statistics. When they bring their
problems they're a lot more vague. You've stated them coherently —
you know what you're looking for, so that wasn't a typical
consultation. But I like these case histories. I don't know how you
got them, but I'd like a copy. They weren't written by a biologist —
I shouldn't think they'd been near one, but anyone should be able
to understand them. I could use these.

'Is it anything like this one?' I could ask them. These cover most
cases. Of course if I do it for real I have to explain everything, and tell
them which routines to use and what they expect to get out. That
takes ages.'

Chris gave Joe a copy of the case histories, asking him to give
him any comments he had or any other cases he thought of.
The summary of his findings was:

1) The researchers needed consultations for education, confidence-
building and advice.
2) An expert system could be developed to address a subset of the
more common problems. This would relieve Joe of all except the
more difficult cases, and would be available to all the laboratory
staff.
3) There was a strong possibility that an expert system shell could
be used.
4) An expert system would be costly at first, but cheaper than
employing another expert in the long run. There was evidence
that Joe had special expertise related to the laboratories; other
resident statisticians could not solve the problems as efficiently.

Bill read the report, and called a meeting. The project was given approval, and Chris was instructed to report back in six months' time. Part-time programming help was available for that time period, Joe was more enthusiastic about the prospects of the project and pledged his help and support; Dave was very keen to see the work under way. Bill was not prepared to commit himself to the amount of money available for software; no extra finance was available for hardware.

KNOWLEDGE ACQUISITION

Chris spent some time reading through the literature he had received about available software. He arranged visits to some companies and a couple of universities, and took Joe with him to see demonstrations. One shell seemed particularly suitable. At the same time Chris was organizing the material he had obtained from his interviews. He set up a database on the computer, cataloguing terms and definitions, and cross-referencing them to transcripts, case studies and books. This was the start of his knowledge base.

Bill agreed to the purchase of the shell. Fortunately a version existed for the computer in use at the centre. Joe independently drew up a list of six types of problems which he thought the expert system should be able to deal with. He also listed out the statistical assumptions necessary for these tests, and any constraints. Chris added these to his database.

Joe continued to work on this approach, helped by Chris. He produced a very detailed breakdown of the six tests he had chosen, working back from the tests to the elementary questions he would ask the scientist. When the shell arrived Chris and his programmer implemented this model. Within a month they had a simple expert system working.

PROBLEMS

There was great excitement at this news, and Chris and Joe decided to compare the program with Joe's real consultations. When Chris sat in on one of these live interviews he was dismayed to learn that the program behaved quite differently from Joe. The program asked a series of relatively technical questions: Joe did not. Joe let the scientists describe their experiment and tentative results. Then he outlined a couple of similar experiments and asked which one was most like the new one. Once a suitable model had

157

been chosen Joe described the purpose of that experiment
and statistical test, and the assumptions made. If the
scientists agreed that this still matched their problem then
Joe told them how to do the test and how to interpret the
results. This process continued until the scientists had
selected a suitable model. The process could take well over
an hour as Joe kept explaining and illustrating until the
scientists understood what he meant. The expert system was
unacceptable — it did not behave like Joe at all.

A REASONABLE SYSTEM

Chris realized that it was impossible to continue without
several transcripts of consultations. The analogies and
examples used by Joe were a critical part of the process.
Joe had not been aware of this, and so had omitted it, but
the explanations, tailored to the scientists' needs and
understanding, were exactly what was needed. Joe was very
sensitive to the scientists' reactions, and frequently altered
the level of explanation. The first expert system was
abandoned, although not deleted, and Chris collected more
transcripts. These were all typed into a wordprocessor.
Chris then edited them, extracting examples and
explanations. He collected these together keeping cross-
references back to the original text. He and the programmer
matched these with the statistical information from the first
model. The process was long and tedious, and models had to
be discussed with Joe. However, after two months, another
working system was available. This system was less
adventurous, but was full of examples and different levels
of explanation.

Now it was possible to compare the behaviour of the
program with real consultations. Results were reasonable,
and a demonstration was given to Joe and Dave. The
consequences of this demonstration were surprising. When
the biologists heard about this informative program they
asked to be allowed to experiment with it. What was even
more surprising was that Joe demanded that he be shown
how to use the shell to modify 'his' system. Over the
following month the biologists spent hours inventing
experiments and discussing them with 'an expert who didn't
always know, but never got bored or irritated'. Joe found
time to sit over the program refining it to make it more like

himself. He also incorporated some of the original case studies. He said that the program helped him to categorize the problems in his own mind.

At the end of the six months' period a simple expert system was made generally available. Requests were made for the following:

1) The inclusion of more types of problem.
2) The facility to call up the statistical routines and, if possible, interpret the results.
3) The enhancement of the interface to allow more natural dialogue.

Cotting Hospital

Cotting Hospital is renowned for its standards in training clinicians and also medical research. Barbara works in the technical support department. About half of her time is spent advising colleagues in their use of computer hardware and software, and providing programming skills. She can devote any spare time to research and development provided that her work is relevant to the clinicians in the hospital. This work is restricted by a low budget and the available computer resources, but she is particularly interested in the problems of diagnosis and recording patients' case notes.

INITIAL REACTIONS TO EXPERT SYSTEMS

Barbara read about expert systems in a medical journal. With her background in mathematical logic and her interest in diagnosis she was fascinated by the possible use of computers to assist the doctors in both training and diagnosis. She spent a lot of her time reading published results from medical research. At first she was interested in the idea of recording consultations between doctors and patients and then analysing the transcripts to design an expert system.

However, when she discussed these plans with the doctors she was disappointed by their reactions. Most of them were sceptical about the feasibility of using computers, others believed that it was either impossible or unethical, and a few refused to get involved owing to a fear that the intention was to replace them by machines. The doctor who was most interested was genuinely too busy to be able to help her. He did send along two of his junior doctors, but although they had more time they had no true commitment to the plans. Against this background the doctors were reluctant to allow tape-recording of their consultations, and refused to allow Barbara access to the confidential case notes. Barbara decided that it would be foolish to try to analyse any consultations if she were not able to look at the case histories of those patients.

Despite this unenthusiastic reaction, Barbara was still confident that she could be of use to the doctors. As she considered the problem of obtaining the case histories she came across an interesting set of published results. These comprised a set of over 100 case notes from patients complaining of abdominal pain including the recorded symptoms, and the correct diagnoses. According to these results the symptoms, as recorded, were sufficient to derive the correct diagnosis.

Barbara decided to work from these findings and produce something for the doctors to see.

A PROBABILITY MODEL

Using methods outlined in books and technical papers, Barbara designed a simple program to diagnose abdominal pain given data about symptoms. This model used probability and was based on Bayes theorem. She was able to estimate most of the probabilities from the set of examples, and obtained estimates for others in a short consultation with one of the doctors.

This work took about three months, and once the program was working she arranged a demonstration for the doctors. They were fairly interested, and keen to run the program with their own invented cases. In particular a group of three doctors spent a couple of hours running the program. Their comments were critical, but constructive. The main criticism was that the program could predict an incorrect diagnosis and give it a high probability value like 98%.

'That wouldn't be too bad if the diagnosis was right', they said. 'But that isn't how we do it. We are not usually that dogmatic, and we would normally consider more than one diagnosis. At the end of a consultation we might have two possible diagnoses in mind, but opt for one of them because of more evidence. You can seldom be absolutely sure just from the symptoms you have used.'

DISCUSSION OF EXAMPLES

Encouraged by this interest Barbara described the set of published examples to these three doctors. They each agreed to diagnose them from the recorded symptoms in order to assess the adequacy of the documented details. To Barbara's surprise their success rates in this diagnosis were all under 60%. They were ready to defend this anomaly. 'The information recorded is totally inadequate. For example, what does "severe" mean when applied to the pain. Is that the patient's definition of severe, or the clinician's definition? Also, the severity might depend on the diagnosis you thought most likely at the time. These summaries don't really tell us enough.'

Based on this, the doctors altered the examples, adding comments and changing entries, until they were happy with them. Barbara listened carefully to these conversations and arguments, noting down their reasoning and the ways in which they considered more than one diagnosis and how they ranked them.

The doctors said that they were happy to do this because it helped them to clarify in their minds how they dealt with more difficult examples and highlighted the importance of clear and complete note-taking during consultations. Once they had reached agreement on the example set they believed that they had gained all the possible benefit from Barbara's work.

FUZZY INDUCTION

By this stage Barbara was committed to the project. The enhanced example set, together with her copious notes, contained a wealth of information. She studied and re-studied her notes in the belief that in order to succeed she had to represent the doctors' methods of handling uncertainty, and ranking diagnoses.

Barbara realized that induction could be used to discover knowledge from her examples, but she knew that a rule induction system would give results which were too crisp, and have similar problems to the first program. Somehow she had to use induction which included uncertainty as an intrinsic part of the data and reasoning.

Over the next couple of months Barbara devised her own inductive system, based on fuzzy logic. Her method analysed the example set and determined which groups of symptoms were indicative of a particular diagnosis, and which were counter-indicative. These induced results could be used to predict diagnoses for other examples. Fuzzy values input in answer to questions about symptoms were used to determine which question to ask next, and the collective set of input values was used to weigh up the relative possibilities of different diagnoses at each stage, until one diagnosis ranked sufficiently high.

Barbara implemented her method on the computer. Bearing in mind the scepticism of some of the doctors, she included output information to the user as the program ran. This information summarized the intermediate possibility values of diagnoses as the program analysed each reply. This showed the way in which answers to questions influenced the process, and also how one diagnosis gained precedence over the others. This implementation took two and a half months.

DOCTOR INVOLVEMENT

When the doctors saw this new program, one of them was very enthusiastic. Although he did not understand how the program worked he was happy about the information it gave, and acknowledged that its handling of symptoms and diagnoses was very similar to his. He interpreted the output values as probabilities rather than fuzzy possibility values, but Barbara did not consider this to be a major problem.

The main fault with the program was that it dealt with only a few diagnoses. The doctor freely admitted that specialists tend to become over-specialized, but he thought that the domain of the program was too restrictive. 'To take a typical case', he argued 'You would consider gynaecological problems if the patient were female. This program doesn't even ask about the sex of the patient.'

ENHANCEMENTS

The doctor agreed that if some improvement could be made to the program, then it would be very useful for training. He was less confident about its usefulness in assisting experienced doctors. He offered to spend some time with Barbara describing modifications which he considered necessary. These fell into three main categories:

162

1) improving the interface between the user and the program,
2) widening the scope of the program,
3) extending the analysis to include knowledge about the risk associated with particular diagnoses, and therefore advice about action to be taken.

Overview

These two case studies illustrate quite different approaches owing to the availability of the experts in each case. However, each follows the general stages outlined in early chapters, although the knowledge engineers used different methods to overcome the problems peculiar to their projects. This versatility and willingness to try different methods distinguishes good knowledge engineers from poor ones.

One important feature of both case studies is that the systems were conceived to overcome known problems. In one case it was the unavailability of an expert, and in the other it was a general lack of understanding about the process of diagnosis. Although the second project did not result in a working expert system, one of the main benefits of the work was that it encouraged the clinicians to think more about their methods of taking case histories and diagnosis, and to overcome any apparent deficiencies. This aspect of expert system development must be stressed. In many projects the production of a working expert system can be secondary compared with the increased awareness and efficiency of the experts. The development of a project can assist an expert to evaluate what he does, discuss and compare his ideas with other experts and an independent knowledge engineer, and then in the light of this increased awareness of his knowledge improve his own methods. This can mean that the expert is subsequently both more efficient and more able to train or coach students or trainees.

The message of this chapter is optimistic. There are many tools available, and the benefits from undertaking knowledge acquisition are great. The cautionary warning is that a project must be useful, not an academic exercise, and that the development team must be willing to throw away ideas which did not work and persevere with different suggestions. Above all, the initial enthusiasm must be maintained throughout development.

Finally . . .

This book has identified problems and suggested approaches. It may be that the nature of this sort of work means that no single methodology can be established. If so, the initiative will lie with the knowledge engineer and his team. There are exciting possibilities for sensible projects, and such projects form a challenge for the engineer. If a methodology is developed then I trust that it will be published quickly and consequently be available to us all. Until then these ideas may prove useful. Good luck in your project — may you enjoy the challenge as much as I do.

Bibliography and references

This bibliography lists journals and books which are relevant. Many of the books contain detailed information on topics mentioned in the text.

Journals

Expert Systems (The International Journal of Knowledge Engineering)
Data and Knowledge Engineering
International Journal of Man-Machine Studies
Cognitive Science
Artificial Intelligence
Fuzzy Sets and Systems

Books

ARTIFICIAL INTELLIGENCE
Texts on the methods and uses of artificial intelligence are:

Elithorn, A.; Banerji, R. *Artificial and Human Intelligence* Elsevier, North Holland, 1984.
O'Shea, T.; Eisenstadt, M. *Artificial Intelligence Tools, Techniques and Applications* Harper and Row, New York, 1984.
Rich, E. *Artificial Intelligence* McGraw-Hill, 1984.
Winston, P.H. *Artificial Intelligence* Addison-Wesley, 1984.

ISSUES INVOLVED IN USES OF ARTIFICIAL INTELLIGENCE

Feigenbaum, E.A.; McCorduck, P. *The Fifth Generation* Pan Books, London, 1984 (a very readable introduction).
Michie, D.; Johnston, R. *The Creative Computer* Pelican, England, 1985 (a book of ideas and some speculation).

165

Yazdani, M.; Narayanan, A. *Artificial Intelligence — Human Effects* Ellis Horwood, 1984 (a very good discussion of some of the implications of current research).

EXPERT SYSTEMS

Alty, J.L.; Coombs, M.J. *Expert Systems, Concepts and Examples* NCC, England, 1984 (an easy introductory book).

Goodall, A. *The Guide to Expert Systems* Learned Information, England, 1985 (a readable guide and overview of the current state of development).

Hayes Roth, F.; Waterman, D.A.; Lenat, D.B. *Building Expert Systems* Addison-Wesley, 1983 (an excellent text).

Michie, D. *Introductory Readings in Expert Systems* Gordon and Breach, London, 1982.

SYSTEMS ANALYSIS

Gane, C.; Sarson, T. *Structured Systems Analysis: Tools and Techniques* Prentice Hall, 1979 (a very good text describing the use of structured English, data flow diagrams, data analysis, data dictionary, etc.).

KNOWLEDGE ACQUISITION

Many of the books mentioned touch on the subject of knowledge acquisition and the knowledge engineer. In particular:

Feigenbaum, E.A.; McCorduck, P. *The Fifth Generation* Pan Books, London, 1984 (gives a description of the work of a famous knowledge engineer, Penny Nii).

Welbank, M. *A review of knowledge acquisition techniques for expert systems* British Telecommunications Research Laboratories Technical Report, Martlesham Heath, Ipswich, England, 1983.

RESULTS FROM PSYCHOLOGY

Ellis, B. *Rational Belief Systems* Basil Blackwell, 1979.

Johnson-Laird, P.N.; Wason, P.C. *Thinking: Readings in Cognitive Science* Cambridge University Press, Cambridge, 1977 (contains some excellent material including heuristics and biases used in reasoning, and problems with probability).

Lehrer, K. *Knowledge* Oxford University Press, 1974.

Newell, A.; Simon, H.A. *Human Problem Solving* Prentice Hall, 1972 (a very detailed study which includes details of experiments and protocol analysis).

Osborn, A.F. *Applied Imagination* Scribner, New York, 1953.

Puff, C.R. *Handbook of Research Methods in Human Memory and Cognition* Academic Press, 1982.

Scholz, R.W. *Decision Making Under Uncertainty* North Holland, 1983 (a very good discussion of problems with established methods of decision analysis).

PROBABILITY AND STATISTICS

Ehrenberg, A.S.C. *A Primer in Data Reduction* John Wiley, 1982 (an excellent text which is easy to read).

REASONING AND LOGIC

Cohen, P.R. *Heuristic Reasoning about Uncertainty: an Artificial Intelligence Approach* Pitman, London, 1985 (the research on endorsements and the SOLOMON project).

Mamdani, E.H.; Gaines, B.R. *Fuzzy Reasoning and its Applications* Academic Press, London, 1981 (some very good examples of the uses of fuzzy logic).

Polya, G. Mathematics and Plausible Reasoning: Vol 2. *Patterns of Plausible Inference* Princetown University Press, 1969 (an excellent text pioneering work on qualitative patterns of reasoning).

Quine, W.V. *Methods of Logic* Routledge and Kegan Paul, 1972 (a formal text on logic).

Van Ryzin, J. *Classification and Clustering* Academic Press, 1977 (contains examples of the uses of fuzzy sets and fuzzy logic).

INDUCTION

Breiman, L.; Friedman, J.H.; Olshen, R.A.; Stone, C.J. *Classification and Regression Trees* Wadsworth International, Belmont, California, 1984 (an excellent text apparently ignored by workers in artificial intelligence; it describes inductive methods from a statistical viewpoint).

Cohen, P.R.; Feigenbaum, E.A. *The Handbook of Artificial Intelligence, Vol 3* Pitman, 1982 (contains a survey of inductive techniques).

Michie, D. *Expert Systems in the Microelectronic Age* Edinburgh University Press, Edinburgh, 1979 (contains a description of Quinlan's ID3 algorithm).

Michie, D. *et al. Machine Intelligence, Vol 8* Ellis Horwood, 1977 (includes a survey of inductive methods).

Sneath, P.H.; Sokal, R.R. *Numerical Taxonomy* W.H. Freeman & Co., San Francisco, 1973 (results from taxonomy which are relevant to inductive methods).

REPERTORY GRID TECHNIQUES

Kelly, G.A. *The Psychology of Personal Constructs* Norton, New York, 1955 (the original work by George Kelly).

Shaw, M.L.G. *Recent Advances in Personal Construct Technology* Academic Press, New York, 1981.

Shaw, M.L.G.; McKnight, C. *Think Again* Prentice Hall, New Jersey, 1981 (a very simple text with examples).

Glossary

artificial intelligence (AI)

The science of trying to make computers perform tasks
which would require intelligence if done by a human being.

average or **mean**

The expected value of a random variable. It is a constant for
a given distribution, and often estimated by the arithmetic
average of values from a sample.

bank

A term used to denote a collection of data, information, or
knowledge.

belief

When dealing with uncertainty one cannot be sure whether
a statement is true or false. The degree of truth is sometimes
measured by a belief factor (see certainty factor, value).

CAD

Computer-aided design.

certainty factor

Some rules or statements may not be absolutely true.
Certainty factors are numerical measures (in some ways
analogous to probabilities) expressing a degree of certainty in
the statement or rule. The system must have a way of
combining these factors in order to make inferences.

classes

For problems such as categorization or classification the

decisions are often referred to as classes. This is also true for the decisions in induction.

cluster analysis

A statistical technique used for classification work. Given several measurements describing a set of individuals a measure of similarity is defined to determine how similar are pairs of individuals. The set is then successively grouped so that individuals which are more alike appear in the same group. This builds a classification or taxonomy for the set.

conceptual model

Before knowledge is entered onto a computer it is necessary to construct a model of the knowledge and how it is used. This can be a diagram, rules, etc. and later forms the basis of the model which is actually implemented.

conditional probability

The conditional probability of A given B is the probability that A occurs given that we know B occurs. In general it will be different from Prob(A).

construct

A term used in the repertory grid technique. A construct is a type of attribute or characteristic which the person chooses to describe the world.

continuous random variable

A random variable which is not discrete. It can take values over a range of real numbers, e.g. between 0 and 1.

correlation coefficient

A statistical measure of the relationship between two random variables. It measures the degree of linear relationship.

critical incident technique

A form of questioning used in psychology. The person is encouraged to describe feelings or anything else he can recall about the incident of concern. By recalling critical incidents he is more likely to remember details of the incident.

decision tree

A decision tree is made up of nodes and branches. It is used to describe concepts or decision-making processes. Often the nodes represent attributes and the branches the various values which the attributes can take.

declarative knowledge

Forms of knowledge which make assertions about entities and the relationships between them, i.e. about states of the world.

declarative language

A computer language which expresses facts and relations rather than procedures. An example is PROLOG, which is logic-based.

discrete random variable

A random variable whose possible values can be listed, e.g. one which can take whole numbers as values.

element

A term used in the repertory grid technique to describe a key example cited by the person.

endorsement

The certainty or belief in a statement may depend on various factors. Endorsements are the record of these factors, i.e. reasons for belief.

expert system

A program containing knowledge from a restricted domain, which uses complex inferential reasoning to carry out tasks which a human expert could do.

expert system shell

An expert system emptied of any knowledge related to any particular domain. It can be used for many different applications if the relevant knowledge can be entered into its structure. EMYCIN is the shell derived from MYCIN.

factor analysis

A statistical method of classification often used by psychologists. It is similar to *principal component analysis*, but makes assumptions about the way in which observed variables are influenced by the underlying factors.

focused grid

A term used in the context of the repertory grid. An elicited grid is reorganized so that similar elements are near to each other, and so are similar constructs. It is used to suggest patterns or relationships.

functional analysis

Knowledge engineering involves an analysis of the way in which the expert *uses* the knowledge; this is sometimes called functional analysis.

heuristic

A rule of thumb. It has no guarantee of success, but usually proves useful.

inductive algorithm

The method which a computer program uses to learn rules or concepts from a training set of examples.

inference mechanism

The part of an expert system which makes inferences from the data and knowledge. It may use inexact reasoning or certainty factors.

inference network

A knowledge representation involving statements and rules. In diagrammatic form the statements are boxes and the rules are lines connecting the boxes. The diagram indicates how the truth of one assertion influences the truth of others.

information retrieval

The process of locating information which has been classified and stored in some ordered manner, typically in a database.

IKBS

Intelligent knowledge based system. A program containing knowledge which can perform tasks which require intelligence if done by humans. The term includes expert systems.

input/output interface

A subpart of any computer system whereby the user communicates with the system, typically by questions and answers. It is a necessary part of an expert system.

knowledge base

A collection of facts, relations, procedures etc., which constitute the knowledge about a particular domain. Part of an expert system.

knowledge dictionary

A systematic catalogue of the various elements of knowledge and the relationships between them. It can be held on a card index or a computer database.

knowledge engineer

A person analogous to the systems analyst, who questions the expert to help to draw up a model of the knowledge, and then suggests representations of it in an expert system.

machine induction

The process whereby a computer program learns rules or concepts from examples presented to it.

mean see *average*

mutually exclusive

Two events are mutually exclusive if the occurrence of one precludes the occurrence of the other, i.e. they cannot both occur.

normal distribution

A statistical distribution commonly used to model a continuous random variable.

173

personal construct theory

A theory from psychology describing the way in which each individual personally constructs a view of reality.

principal component analysis

A statistical method of classifying individuals where there are several measurements on each individual.

procedural knowledge

Knowledge describing what to do, i.e. procedures. It forms instructions of what to do with facts etc.

relative frequency

If an experiment is performed N times, and outcome A occurs n times, then the relative frequency of A is n/N. This is often used to estimate the value Prob(A).

repertory grid technique

A tool used by psychologists to represent a person's view of a problem in terms of elements and constructs.

rule-based programs

Rules of the form 'IF condition THEN consequence' are a simple and common representation of knowledge. The consequence may be a fact or action. Programs which hold knowledge in this form are called rule-based systems or production systems.

Shannon's information statistic

A numerical measure of the amount of information in a set of data. It is related to entropy, and used in the ID3 algorithm to measure how well an attribute discriminates between classes.

significance

The result of a statistical test is said to be (highly) significant if it was (highly) unlikely to have happened by chance. A significant result often leads to the rejection of a null hypothesis in favour of an alternative.

174

spread

The spread or variability of a distribution measures how likely it is to get a value away from the mean. If the variability is high then it is likely that the random variable will have a value far from the mean.

structured English

A subset of English which states rules and conditions in a precise form. It is used to write specifications for programs in systems analysis.

systems analysis

The process of investigating a system, evaluating its strengths and weaknesses, and specifying and designing a new system to meet predefined objectives.

training set

A set of examples or case histories, produced by the expert and presented to an inductive system in order to discover rules.

value

The relevance of a statement depends not only on the level of belief but also on the risk or value associated with it. A condition may be highly important even if unlikely.

variability see *spread*

Index

177